Fatal Attractions

Erin Butler

Published by Trellis Publishing, 2021.

FATAL ATTRACTIONS

First edition. July 7, 2021.

Copyright © 2021 Erin Butler.

ISBN: 979-8224101757

Written by Erin Butler.

FATAL ATTRACTIONS

ERIN BUTLER

CAROLYN WARMUS

Carolyn Warmus is serving a sentence of 25 years to life in Bedford Hills Correctional Facility for Women for murdering the wife of her lover, a fellow elementary school teacher.

Her case was widely referred to in the media as the "Fatal Attraction murder" in reference to the 1987 movie.

She was 25 years old at the time of the murder in 1989, and 28 when she was convicted in 1992 after two trials.

Neighbors and acquaintances, from her time in Michigan and New York, described her as pleasant and sunny. One was quoted as saying she was the kind of girl you could take home to Mom.

But people who knew her better said that her big grin hid an emotionally disturbed, depressed, and occasionally suicidal individual.

In her 20's, blond, wide-eyed Carolyn had a sexy personality, a great figure, and dressed expensively and fashionably. She turned heads. Her employers described her as cheerful and very competent. But she had also begun obsessing over a string of older unavailable men and, by the time of the murder, had a long history of bizarre behavior—some of it criminal—in relation to these romantic entanglements.

Early life

Carolyn Warmus was born on January 8, 1964. She was the eldest of three children of millionaire Thomas Warmus and his wife Elizabeth. The family lived in small affluent neighborhoods around Troy, Michigan, a suburb of Detroit.

In 1958, Thomas Warmus had begun a career as a life insurance agent. In 1963, he formed the American Way Service Corporation, which later became a holding company for a number of insurance companies. He was a millionaire by the time he was raising his family.

Carolyn and her younger sister and brother—Tracey and Tommy—had a typical wealthy upbringing and lifestyle. They were not lacking in material comforts.

However, a family acquaintance told People Magazine in 1990 that there was no deep emotional bond between the parents and their children. A childhood friend told People that none of the children had a good relationship with their father, who was obsessed with business and a rich lifestyle. Their mother was also more interested in being a socialite than in being a mother.

Elizabeth Warmus filed for divorce in 1970. The Warmus' marriage had been difficult for years. When they divorced in 1972, Carolyn was eight years old. By this time, American Way Service Corp. was worth $107 million.

Thomas Warmus married his secretary, Nancy, who was younger and wore mink coats, tight strapless sequined dresses, and liked expensive sports cars.

Elizabeth won custody of the children and they lived with her in Birmingham, Michigan, another Detroit suburb. Thomas built Nancy a huge fenced-in house on a hill in the new-money neighborhood of Franklin Village.

When Carolyn was 14, Elizabeth remarried and moved to the East Coast. The children did not go with her. They moved to the big house in Franklin Village. Carolyn told a friend that the house was always empty. She and Tracey used it to throw lavish parties.

High school

Carolyn attended Seaholm High School and graduated in 1981 with honors. She was athletic, cheerful, blond and attractive, got good grades, and played on the basketball team.

Peers who knew her well said that her sunny façade hid deep emotional problems caused by the bitter divorce of her parents and lack of affection from her parents, especially her father.

She and her sister were rivals. Tracey was more popular and better looking, which Carolyn found upsetting.

Schoolmates who were interviewed for a February 1990 People Magazine article painted a disturbing picture of the teenaged Carolyn.

They said she tried to buy popularity and affection by inviting people to her family's Florida home, throwing extravagant parties, and throwing cash around. In her senior year, she paid a classmate $100 to set her up with a guy she had her eye on.

The $100 date told People his involvement with Carolyn lasted a few months, and he was happy to get her out of his life when it ended. He described her as an extremely unhappy person who complained about having no father and no affection. He said she sometimes talked about suicide.

University of Michigan

After high school, Carolyn attended the University of Michigan and graduated in 1985 with a Bachelor of Science (Psychology). She was already a very troubled person by the time she went to college and became increasingly so. Friends who knew her in college said that suffered from depression and occasionally spoke of suicide.

Some of her acquaintances told police later that she was "ditzy" and "schizo."

While attending university, Carolyn had a series of relationships with older men who were attached that ended badly and left her feeling like a victim. She was apparently incapable of maintaining a successful relationship, and she behaved obsessively during and after her entanglements.

It has been theorized that her attraction to these unattainable men, and her going to extremes to get them back after they broke up with her—or to get back at them—stemmed from her poor relationship with her father. She was, after all, desirable enough to interest any attainable man she wanted.

Paul Laven

In February 1983, while attending the University of Michigan, Carolyn met a teaching assistant named Paul Laven. By June, they were dating.

According to people who knew them, he was never serious about her, but she was obsessed with him. In everything she did, she had him in mind. If someone paid her a compliment about an outfit or a hairdo, she would ask them what Paul would think of it.

Paul Laven broke up with Carolyn in December and soon announced his engagement to another student, Wendy Siegel.

Carolyn began stalking and harassing the couple. Records from a court complaint filed by Paul show that Carolyn's behavior became obsessive and disturbing. The way she later described the situation to private investigator Jim Russo was that she had tried and tried to win him back after he married someone else and it hadn't worked.

She followed Paul around campus, harassed him at his office, and phoned him day and night.

The couple moved to another town and got an unlisted phone number.

On April 6, Carolyn conned a phone company employee into giving her that unlisted number. On April 10, she entered Paul and Wendy's apartment and had to be removed by police. She had also been harassing Paul at his office.

In May 1984, she left a note on Paul's car claiming that she was pregnant with his baby and begging him to phone her.

After returning from a vacation in Florida, Carolyn left Wendy a deliberately misspelled note that said she hoped Wendy had enjoyed the past week of Carolyn not bothering her because now she could start worrying again since Carolyn was back.

She added that Wendy would have even more to compete with now, because of Carolyn's tan. That gives some insight into Carolyn's mind: she thought a tan was relevant.

She went on to say that, of course, "with a body like mine" Wendy had to realize what tough competition she was up against, that Wendy was now just about out of the running completely, and that Paul would probably continue to pretend to care about Wendy as long as she let him live with her.

Laven and Siegel were granted a temporary restraining order against Warmus two weeks before their July 1984 wedding to prevent her from wrecking their wedding or reception.

After their wedding, they obtained a permanent order restraining Warmus from communicating with them "forever" and from interfering with their "rights of privacy" and their "rights to travel."

Carolyn's family was Catholic, but she had begun taking instruction to convert to Judaism while she was dating Paul Laven, who was Jewish. She converted to Judaism in her final semester, which was almost a year after Laven and Siegel were married.

Her instructor, Rabbi David Nelson of the Congregation Beth Shalom, Oak Park, described Carolyn as intelligent and quiet.

He assumed she was taking instruction in order to marry a Jewish husband, but noted that she was never accompanied to her classes by anyone. This was unusual. She attended her conversion ceremony alone as well, which he said was very unusual.

Carolyn chose the Hebrew name Chana Ariela, "gracious lioness of god."

Summer after graduating from University of Michigan

After Carolyn graduated from the University of Michigan, she moved back to the home of her father and stepmother in Franklin Village and spent the summer of 1985 preparing to move to New York.

She found a summer job as a waitress at a nightclub in Royal Oak, Michigan, called the Juke Box. It was a rock and roll bar where booze was cheap and the pretty waitresses danced on the bar for the patrons.

In the opinion of Peter Sherman, bouncer, Carolyn fit right in. She had a great smile, a great figure, and a great attitude. She was never in a bad mood, he said.

Credit Cards

The bar manager, Debbie Mullin, said that Carolyn was pulling off credit card fraud while she worked at the Juke Box. She was ultimately fired for it. Federal investigators investigated, but Warmus was never prosecuted because the investigators couldn't find enough evidence to make the charges stick.

According to Mullin, Carolyn used a classic trick: she would run a card through the credit card imprinting machine two or three times, use one imprint for the real credit card customer, and use the others for customers who paid cash. She would then keep the cash instead of putting it in the cash register.

Brian "Buddy" Fetter

Carolyn met a businessman named Brian Fetter, nicknamed Buddy, while working at the Juke Box. They had dated. Bouncer Peter Sherman said that Fetter showed up one day to ask what the heck was going on with Carolyn.

According to Sherman, Fetter told him that she had been hounding him. She had been leaving him so many phone messages that he had been forced to change his number. That was when Sherman first realized there was something truly off about Carolyn.

NYC, Master's Degree, Parco and Russo and the married bartender

Carolyn moved to New York City in 1985 after leaving the Juke Box. She earned a Master's degree in elementary education in 1987 at Teacher's College, Columbia University. In New York, her pattern of relationships with inappropriate men and stalking continued.

She was living in Manhattan when she had an affair with a married bartender who lived and worked in New Jersey.

One afternoon in the summer of 1987, Carolyn waltzed into the office of Vincent Parco, the private investigator who later testified about having sold Warmus a gun. She had apparently found him in the yellow pages.

Parco was a man who lived large and loved to be around young women. Carolyn looked prim but hot in a white tennis outfit. Parco's investigative specialty was sniffing out illegal tenants, but Warmus wanted to put her married bartender under surveillance.

Parco assigned Jim Russo to the case. Carolyn wanted to go along on the mission. This was not standard operating procedure, but Russo brought her along.

They drove to the bartender's house and then to the Ramada where he worked. The bar was not busy enough for Russo to take pictures without being noticed. Back in the car with Warmus, Russo found her pleasant, vivacious, and talkative. She asked him if he was married and if his wife minded his long hours.

She talked about herself. She talked about a man she had been seeing in Michigan who had married somebody else. She talked about how she had tried so hard to get that man back but nothing worked. She talked about the new boyfriend—the bartender—and how everything was finally okay because of him.

Then the reason for the surveillance came out. The bartender had promised to leave his wife for Carolyn and he was too slow about it. Carolyn wanted to send the bartender's wife some compromising photos that would move the situation along. (Possibly, the bartender had never made any such promise, in good faith or bad, but had simply tired of her.)

Russo was not able to catch the bartender doing anything incriminating. The surveillance was a bust. According to Russo, Parco and Warmus then cooked up a scheme to solve that problem. They could superimpose photos of Carolyn in sexy poses on photos of the bartender.

Russo claimed he would not have gone along with faking evidence, but he was willing to take riské pictures of Warmus. She posed in a variety of sexual poses in see-through outfits and skimpy lingerie while Russo took photos.

He delivered the film to Parco.

According to Russo, a few days later he saw evidence on Parco's desk that Parco and Warmus were trying to put together a cut-and-paste with the photos of Carolyn and photos that someone else had taken of the bartender.

That plan also seems to have been a bust. It might have worked out if Photoshop had existed back then. Maybe Carolyn had already lost interest in the bartender and his wife and abandoned the plan.

After that, Russo saw Warmus around Parco's office a couple of times a week for a while. He suspected that the relationship between Warmus and Parco became intimate at some point.

Forgery

In Carolyn's murder trials, the issue of forged telephone records came up. The prosecution tried to introduce a previous instance of Carolyn committing forgery.

In June 1987, a woman was involved in car accident and identified herself to the other driver as Carolyn Warmus. Later, to establish an alibi against the subsequent damage claim, Carolyn wrote to the other driver stating that on the day of the collision she had been a chaperone on a school trip out of state.

She included a letter signed by school official Dr. Richard Sprague to back up her claim. The lawyer for the other side of the damage claim dropped the case.

Later, while following Warmus' trial, that lawyer sent a copy of the letter to Dr. Sprague. Sprague said he had not written the letter, the signature was not his, that particular school trip did not occur on that date, and Carolyn was not on that trip when it did occur.

She certainly could not have been on a school trip in June 1987, since she wasn't hired by the Westchester County school system until September.

Carolyn's trial judge refused to allow the letter into evidence on grounds that it would be too prejudicial.

Westchester County School System

In September 1987, after getting her Master's Degree, Carolyn was hired by the public elementary school system of Westchester County, New York. She served as a substitute for teachers on maternity leave. She also began work on her Doctorate of Education at Columbia.

After her time working as a substitute, she was hired without reservation by the Byram Hills school district to work at Coman Hill Elementary School.

The personnel director of Byram Hills, Dr. Linda Ochser, told The New York Times that she was impressed by Carolyn's academic credentials and that Carolyn had sailed through their interview process as an outstanding candidate. Dr. Ochser described Warmus as a "very vivacious, upbeat teacher."

But some of Carolyn's co-workers later told police that she was a nut and had several personalities.

Greenville School and meeting Paul Solomon

Carolyn's first substitute teaching job was at Greenville Elementary in Scarsdale, New York. Here the 23-year-old met yet another married man, 38-year-old Paul Solomon, also an elementary school teacher. As the more experienced teacher, he has been described as having been her mentor. He has been described as being gentle, understanding, and mentoring towards younger female teachers in general.

It is not known exactly when their relationship became sexual. Paul's wife, Betty Jeanne, did not mention any suspicions to anybody.

Paul testified later that he cared for Carolyn, felt guilty about the sex, wanted to break up with her, wasn't going to divorce his wife, and that he and Warmus had intercourse and oral sex several times throughout the year. "It's very hard to resist Carolyn," he said.

He was drawn to her youth, good looks, taut body, outgoing and fun personality—though he also found her possessive and unpredictable.

Carolyn had a duplex apartment above the Catch A Rising Star comedy club in Manhattan and soon they were meeting there. They also met in hotel rooms and had sex in Carolyn's car.

In December, Carolyn received a card from Paul that said he was falling in love with her.

Another note from Paul said, "If you're smart you'll do one of two things. Turn away and never see me again and save yourself from the pain and hurt, or keep loving me and take the risk of you and I having something together forever."

Around this time, Carolyn told a University of Michigan friend on the phone that she was dating a married man who was going to leave his wife for her.

Warmus' next substitute posting, partly through that school year, was at Pleasantville School. Her relationship with Solomon continued.

Paul and Betty Jeanne

Betty Jeanne's high school sweetheart, Earl, who she had been planning to marry, was killed in a car crash during her freshman year in college. In the spring of 1967, she met Paul Solomon.

College friends describe Betty Jeanne as a happy, agreeable, helpful girl and Paul as intense, competitive, confrontational, and someone who wanted to be important. They say she became quiet and reclusive under his influence.

A former roommate of Betty Jeanne's told New York Magazine that he was domineering, possessive, and jealous, that he told her what to wear, what sorority to join, and what friends to drop.

Another friend told New York Magazine that Betty Jeanne was sweet and Paul was not nice, and added that Paul was rude to Betty Jeanne. Friends were surprised when they married. But Betty Jeanne was in love with Paul.

Their wedding was in 1970. Betty Jeanne had dropped out of school a couple of years earlier. Paul had just left school and joined the Air Force.

Their daughter, Kristan, was born in 1973. Shortly after that, Paul left the Air Force to go back to school and finish his degree. Then he was hired as a teacher at Greenville Elementary School, which was in one of the richest school districts in the country.

Betty Jeanne worked as a bank teller and made her way up the ranks to branch manager. In 1984, she left the bank for a better paying job with a collection agency. They bought their Greenburgh condominium in 1987.

At the time of her 1989 murder, Betty Jeanne was 40 years old and an account executive with Continental Credit Corporation.

The Solomons were comfortable, but they were middle class. Most of Kristan's friends had wealthy parents. The Solomons could not give their daughter all the things her friends had.

To increase their income, Paul started coaching sports throughout the school year and in the summer. He also took up basketball, bowling, and golf to keep fit. Those activities kept him away from home most evenings. Betty Jeanne developed her own interests in addition to her job and got involved in civic activities.

Both of the Solomons were always busy. Their condo was a home for the daughter they both adored, but it also became just a place to grab a meal and go off again.

Paul was a good teacher. Some of his earlier prickliness had softened and he had morphed into a good authority figure for students needing a firm hand.

He insisted on being the authority figure at home as well, though, and Betty Jeanne told her mother she was sick of this. Paul was also still subjecting Betty Jeanne to the occasional rudeness that had made her college friends uncomfortable.

Betty Jeanne considered leaving Paul several times, but she never did. According to testimony in Carolyn's trials, both Paul and Betty Jeanne were having affairs but they were not ready to put an end to their marriage.

Paul and Carolyn and Paul's family

Paul introduced Carolyn to Kristan one evening while he was coaching Kristan's basketball team. Carolyn tried to play a role as a friend of the family or a big sister to Kristan. She gave Kristan expensive gifts and took her shopping. One night, Kristan went to a show in Manhattan with Paul, Carolyn, and another teacher.

In early 1988, all three Solomons were out to dinner with Carolyn when Carolyn offered to take Kristan on a ski trip during the upcoming school break. (Carolyn's University of Michigan freshman yearbook lists her interests as skiing and travel).

Betty Jeanne told her sister Joyce about the planned trip and said that people were teasing her about letting her daughter go on this trip with a bimbo. Joyce wanted to know if Carolyn was afraid they would go bar hopping. But Carolyn told her sister that Carolyn seemed like a nice enough woman, and she didn't want to spoil her daughter's fun.

On that ski trip, Carolyn told Kristan that she was concerned that Betty Jeanne didn't like her very much. Kristan knew that Carolyn was right but kindly tried to persuade her otherwise.

Summer 1988

In the summer of 1988, Paul temporarily broke off his affair with Carolyn.

According to trial testimony, during that summer Carolyn told a Michigan friend Ryan Attenson that "with her money," she and Paul and "Paul's family" would have "a perfect life together." She was going to make sure that she ended up with him. She also told Attenson that she was thinking of hiring a private investigator to prove to Paul that Betty Jeanne was cheating on him.

During that summer of 1988, Carolyn wrote notes to Paul and gave Kristan extravagant presents. For Kristan's birthday in August, Warmus dropped by unexpectedly with a bracelet and two outfits. Kristan later testified that she was hesitant about this visit, because she knew her mom didn't enjoy having Warmus in the house, and she was afraid they would "have words."

Carolyn visited Jim Russo's new office a few times during the summer and fall of 1988. (In February, Russo had left Vincent Parco to form his own investigation firm.)

On one visit, she claimed that one of her father's airplanes had exploded or crashed on a runway and that it was sabotage. On another visit, she said that her sister had been the victim of a hit-and-run driver. Carolyn mentioned a short dark-haired woman in relations to both of these incidents.

Again in Russo's office, a few months before the murder, Warmus told Russo that she had seen this woman before and that the woman's name was "Jean or Betty Jean." Russo testified that Carolyn begged for protection against this woman who was threatening her family. He suggested a bodyguard, but she asked for a gun and a silencer.

According to trial witness Lisa Kattai, Lisa and Carolyn had worked together at a temp job in August 1988 and were friendly. Kattai's driver's license went missing on that job. Carolyn had access to Kattai's purse at the time.

According to her testimony, Kattai's hairstyle in that license photo looked much the same as Warmus' hairstyle at the time the license disappeared. Kattai reported the loss when it happened, and she thought no more of it. She had no opinion as to whether or not Warmus had anything to do with the disappearance of the license.

Later, the prosecution would suggest that Warmus used Kattai's driver's license for I.D. when she bought gun ammunition.

Fall 1988 and early 1989

Paul Solomon and Carolyn Warmus resumed their sexual relationship in the fall of 1988 even though, according to his testimony, he had conflicting feelings and felt guilty.

Vincent Parco testified at trial that Carolyn had hounded him for months before the murder to get her a gun for protection against burglars that were running rampant in her neighborhood. She finally broke through his resistance in the first week of January 1989 and he sold her an unregistered .25 caliber Beretta pistol with bullets and a homemade silencer for $2,500.

Patricia January, a school nurse, testified that a week before the murder Carolyn told her that she owned a gun because living alone was terrifying.

The murder

On January 15, 1989, a Sunday, Kristan was away on a ski trip with friends. Betty Jeanne and Paul were watching TV. Carolyn phoned at 1:37 p.m.

Carolyn wanted to know why Paul hadn't taken her out for her 25th birthday on January 8. They agreed to meet at 7:30 p.m. at Treetops, a restaurant in the Holiday Inn at Yonkers. Paul told Betty Jeanne he was going bowling that night. They had a confrontation about it.

He hooked his car up to a battery charger sometime that afternoon. Since his wife would be staying home that night, he could use her car that evening. (Later, one of the prosecutors, pushing a conspiracy theory, hinted that the battery charger cable was meant to be an arrow to the murder site for a hitman.)

Paul left home around 6:30 p.m., made an appearance at the bowling alley, and left the bowling alley at 7:15 p.m. He drove to Treetops in Betty Jeanne's car and waited for Carolyn.

Shortly before 7:12 p.m., New York Telephone Company operator Linda Viana Newcombe answered a 911 call from a woman in distress. Newcombe was not able to say at trial if the caller had said "he is trying to kill me" or "she is trying to kill me." But she was sure she heard "trying to kill me" before the call went dead.

Newcombe immediately reported the call to police. Sources differ as to whether the operator got the number wrong and therefore reported it to the wrong police detachment, or she got the number right but the reverse directory was not up to date. Either way, the police went to the wrong home, they did not find Betty Jeanne on the living room floor, and they did not save her.

At about 7:45 p.m., Carolyn walked into the Treetops bar to meet up with Paul. They had drinks and a meal. The waitress saw them deep in conversation. They were there for almost two hours.

Paul later told the jury that he told Carolyn she should seek her future elsewhere. He said, "I'd be so happy to dance at your wedding and see you happy." Her answer to that was, "What about your happiness, Paul? Don't you deserve to be happy?" His answer to that was, "If anything happens to Betty Jeanne and me, I'd never get married anyway."

After this effort at pushing her away, he went to the parking lot and sat in Carolyn's car. He allowed her to give him oral sex. In a few minutes, they were finished. They promised to meet again soon and went their separate ways.

At 11:42 p.m., Paul arrived home at his Greenburgh condo and found Betty Jeanne's body on the living room floor. He called the Village of Scarsdale Police Department. "It's my wife! I think she's dead! I need help. My name is Paul Solomon. She's not moving. She's covered with blood! Please hurry!"

Scarsdale Police notified Greenburgh Police who dispatched units to the scene. They found a distraught Paul Solomon and Betty Jeanne lying in a pool of blood.

It was later determined that Betty Jeanne had received nine bullets in her back and legs and had been pistol-whipped about her head.

Nobody had heard the gunshots. The only sign of a struggle was a disconnected phone jack. There was no sign of forced entry. Police photographs of the scene showed a black wool glove near the body. This glove later nailed Carolyn.

Investigation January 1989 - Paul

Paul Solomon was the initial suspect. He admitted to police that he'd had an affair with Carolyn for the past year, that they'd had a date at Treetops after he went to the bowling alley on the night of the murder, and even that they'd had sex in Carolyn's car in the parking lot after the date.

Police had been able to substantiate his alibi of going bowling and then hooking up with Carolyn. The investigators started looking for another suspect.

Very soon, Solomon broke off his relationship with Carolyn again and took up with a new girlfriend, Barbara Ballor.

Investigation January 1989 - Carolyn

Carolyn, on the advice of her father's lawyer Mr. Fiore, took a polygraph test on January 20 as a precautionary measure. It recorded truthful responses when she was asked if she had murdered Betty Jeanne and if she had been in the apartment when Betty Jeanne was murdered.

It was a bit iffy about whether or not she was protecting anyone. Polygraph results are not admissible in court.

Investigation March/April 1989 - Carolyn and phone records and guns

Once Paul had been ruled out, police looked into other options: professional hit, a burglary gone bad, aborted sex crime. By March 1989, none of those had panned out. Eventually, they turned their attention again to Warmus.

Detective Richard Constantino spent two months investigating Carolyn's phone records from immediately before and after the murder. The records revealed that many conversations had taken place between Vincent Parco and Carolyn Warmus immediately before and after the murder.

Parco gave police a series of different reasons for those phone conversations. His stories kept changing. Eventually, he relented and admitted that Carolyn had wanted a gun with a silencer and he had provided them.

Parco's friend George Peters had made the silencer. Peters had test fired the gun into a block of wood in the process of making the silencer, and police matched a casing from his workshop to a casing found next to Betty Jeanne's body.

In addition to all the calls between Warmus and Parco, investigators found a call from Carolyn to a gun store at 3:02 p.m. on the day of Betty Jeanne's murder. Carolyn and Paul had just spoken on the phone at 1:37 p.m. that day and set up their date for later that evening, and Carolyn knew that Kristan out of town skiing.

The gun store was called Ray's Sport Shop and it was in North Plainfield, New Jersey, twenty miles west of Manhattan. Investigators drove to the shop and found that only one person from outside of New Jersey, and only one female—those being the same person—had bought .25 caliber ammunition there that day. That person had used a driver's license in the name of Lisa Kattai for I.D.

Police visited Lisa and she told them about her disappeared driver's license from the previous summer. They soon ascertained that Lisa had not been the purchaser of the ammunition and that she had worked in an office with Carolyn.

June 1989 – stalking again

Carolyn Warmus had begun pursuing Paul Solomon again, soon after the murder. In June 1989, she followed Paul to Puerto Rico.

She didn't realize that Paul was taking the trip with a new girlfriend, Barbara Ballow, in tow.

Doing anything to interject herself into the situation, Carolyn called Ballor's family on the phone. She pretended to be a police officer and began making wild accusations about Ballor in an effort to get them to break up the relationship.

After returning from Puerto Rico, Ballor obtained a protection order against Carolyn Warmus.

August 1989 – hospitalized

On August 8, 1989, Carolyn's neighbors reported bizarre behavior at her Upper East Side Manhattan address, 1485 First Avenue. Officers arrived and found Carolyn to be emotionally disturbed and at risk of harming herself. She was subsequently sent to the psych ward for a week.

Arrest and first indictments (dismissed)

Carolyn Warmus was indicted for second-degree murder and weapons possession on February 2, 1990. On February 6, she was freed on $250,000 bail, the bond having been posted by her father.

On April 4, 1990, Associated Press reported that Warmus' lawyer, David Lewis, had asked for the indictments to be dismissed due to prosecutorial misconduct in the form of grand jury leaks to the press.

On August 7, 1990, The Day, a Connecticut newspaper, reported that Judge John Carey had dismissed the indictments on grounds that the "integrity of the grand jury proceeding was impaired." The reasons given by the judge were that the state had concealed an immunity agreement with a key prosecution witness and that instructions to the grand jury were faulty.

Vincent Parco, who had sold the pistol to Carolyn, had been granted immunity in exchange for his testimony.

First trial

The prosecution obtained a new indictment for second-degree murder against Warmus and, on February 14, 1991, the famous "Fatal Attraction" trial began in White Plains, Westchester County.

Douglas J. Fitzmorris was the prosecutor, David Lewis was Carolyn's defense attorney, and Judge John Carey was again presiding.

Carolyn became a media star with her femme fatale look, sparking the "Fatal Attraction" fascination. She paraded into the courthouse each day in designer clothes and sunglasses, looking like a model. She was all over the newspapers.

The prosecution's evidence included Parco's testimony (under immunity) about the gun and silencer, phone company records of the call to the gun shop, and the use of a stolen I.D. to buy a gun.

The defense was that there was a conspiracy between Paul Solomon and Vincent Parco and they faked evidence against Carolyn.

Some of the evidence included:

Warmus called Parco the day after the murder to say that some teacher had been stabbed or bludgeoned and that she had thrown her gun off the parkway

Parco admitted that he was infatuated with Warmus but he had always rejected her sexual advances

In August 1989 Warmus had asked Parco to check out a license plate number of a woman Solomon had been dating

Warmus had told Parco during the summer of 1989 that she had never had a relationship with Solomon and that she had been bowling "with a bunch of teachers" when Betty Jeanne was killed

A trucker named Anthony Gambino said that Parco had asked him in the summer of 1988 to commit a murder

A guy named Joseph Lisella said he had overheard Parco soliciting a hit

Carolyn's father claimed that Parco had tried to shake him down for a lot of money in the summer of 1989

The defense had a different version of the phone records than the prosecution did, which put in question Carolyn's call to the gun shop and backed up the defense's theory of conspiracy—the judge allowed the jury to have both versions

Paul Solomon's testimony in this trial was undermined when the prosecution elicited the fact that he had signed a movie deal for his story.

The jury deliberated for twelve days before declaring themselves unable to arrive at a unanimous verdict. They were deadlocked at eight to four in favor of conviction. Judge Carey declared a mistrial on April 27, 1991.

The jurors in favor of acquittal said they could not believe that a woman could have been so brutal as to pistol-whip the victim that way. One juror couldn't believe that a woman could hit a moving target nine times. But they all believed that the defense's phone records were forged, possibly out of desperation.

Second trial

The second trial began on January 22, 1992. James A. McCarty was the prosecutor this time, and Carolyn's new defense attorney was William I. Aronwald. Judge John Carey was again in charge of the proceedings.

The new defense approach was about reasonable doubt rather than a frame-up. They still intended to create suspicion of a Parco/Solomon conspiracy, but they knew that the jurors in the first trial had not believed most of the conspiracy evidence.

After the first trial, Carolyn was indicted for the phone records forgery, but the judge disallowed that from being brought into evidence. Why? Because it could have been her team that was responsible for the forgery, not Carolyn, and it was therefore not evidence of consciousness of guilt on her part.

The prosecution's path was the same as before. But they suddenly got a nice surprise.

A black glove that had been in the murder scene police photos, but had later disappeared, had been rediscovered. And Forensics had found finger-shaped bloodstains on the top of this glove.

Foreshadowing the O.J. trial, all manner of evidence was put forth about this glove. Where it was manufactured and who imported it. Who bought it and when. Testimony about fibers and receipts.

Kristan Solomon testified for the prosecution about what kinds of gloves Carolyn normally wore. Carolyn's stepmother Nancy Kay Dailey testified that Carolyn had lots of black gloves.

The New York Times said, "for a minute every eye shifted to the young woman at the defense table in the flowing black skirt and the black boots." Nancy said that black was not among Carolyn's favorite shades. "She looks very good in bright colors."

After the glove thing died away, the trial went back to normal. Someone testified about the silencer. There was testimony to refute the school nurse's assertion that Carolyn had talked about having a gun. The forged phone records were out, so the defense presented some theory about somebody tapping into Carolyn's phone line and making calls on her "behalf."

In summation, the defense powerfully argued that Betty Jeanne was "unwanted baggage" for Paul and also brought up the "magically" materialized glove.

The prosecution powerfully argued that there was too much evidence against Carolyn to be argued away and that Paul had nothing to gain by getting rid of his wife, whereas Carolyn had long viewed Betty Jeanne as an obstacle.

A few other pieces of evidence on the prosecution side were:

Carolyn had just found out that Kristan was away

The Solomons had attended a bar mitzvah the previous day (family thing getting in Carolyn's craw)

Carolyn's phone bill showed a call to the gun shop 30 minutes after she finished speaking to Solomon

Timing: Betty Jeanne died at 7:15; Paul showed up at Treetops on time at 7:30; Carolyn was late at 7:45 and claimed to Paul that traffic was the reason

Conviction

On May 26, 1992, after six days of deliberation, the second jury found Carolyn guilty of second-degree murder and illegal gun possession.

Jury members cited "the glove" as an important reason for their verdict.

Sentence

The minimum sentence possible for this charge was 15 years, but Judge Carey handed Warmus 25 years to life, the maximum. He said that she had committed "a hideous act, a most extreme, illegal and wanton murder."

Sexual abuse in prison and lawsuit

In 2001, a prison guard retired to avoid charges after officials accused him of having an affair with Carolyn.

This was reported by The Post in 1999: Sgt. Dominick Crisafulli, 52, was suspended for engaging in an "inappropriate relationship" with Warmus for nine months.

A stack of letters between them was confiscated, and she apparently had her parents meet him at a restaurant to give him barbecue tools as a gift.

According to The Post, the letters were passed between guard and prisoner by Warmus' private investigator and his wife, a lawyer who works for Warmus. Their visiting privileges were suspended pending the outcome of an investigation.

In April 2004, corrections officer Glenn Looney was charged with second-degree sexual abuse for having sexual contact with Carolyn in 2002. She had reportedly kept his semen refrigerated for two years to back up her accusation.

The case against Looney was about to go to trial in April 2005 when it was abruptly dismissed. Carolyn Warmus was unwilling to go forward with the case, according to a source in the Westchester County D.A.'s office.

In October 2004, Warmus filed a civil action for deprivation of rights against the Bedford Hills Correctional Facility, the New York State Department of Correctional Services, and a list of people associated with those entities. She claimed that she had been forced to have sex with guards in exchange for ordinary privileges and that she was punished with protective custody when she tried to complain.

In December 2009, the Court ordered New York State to "issue a check for $10,000 to Carolyn Warmus for deposit in her inmate account" and to pay her lawyers $69,531.53.

Status now

Carolyn is still incarcerated at the Bedford Hills Correctional Facility for Women. If she had been handed the minimum sentence of 15 years, she would have been paroled in 2007. She will be eligible to apply for parole in 2017. She will be 53.

Update on Carolyn's father

In 1990, The New York Times reported that Mr. Thomas Aloysius Warmus' net worth was more than $150 million. He owned a fleet of jets, several homes, and dozens of cars.

Sometime in the 1990s, he declared bankruptcy for himself and for American Way Service Corp.

In 2002, he was sentenced to 97 months for hiding assets from the bankruptcy proceedings.

"Warmus was found guilty of orchestrating a complex scheme to conceal assets that included high-end collectible automobiles, such as Ferraris and a Lamborghini; a 42-foot yacht; and a collectible World War II fighter aircraft. Before filing for bankruptcy, Warmus had a net worth of $50 million and his insurance companies were valued at more than $100 million. His scheme to defraud creditors began several months pre-petition when he diverted revenues from American Way Service Corp. to companies in the name of his wife and diverted his personal income to companies in the name of his business associates, wife, and mother-in-law. While in bankruptcy, Warmus continued to sell undisclosed assets and use the proceeds for his personal benefit. During the criminal trial, a trial attorney from the Miami office of the U.S. Trustee served as Special Assistant U.S. Attorney and the U.S. Trustee Program's National Bankruptcy Fraud Coordinator testified as an expert on bankruptcy matters."

In 2007, Mr. Warmus' convictions and sentences were affirmed, his appeals came to an end, and he was still incarcerated at that time.

PIN UP QUEEN KILLER :

THE TRUE STORY OF SAMANTHA SCOTT

27

DALE CROWELL

Andrea Claire aka Samantha Scott had was born in 1941 and grew up in New Jersey.

At the age of 15, Andrea claimed that her mother forced her to marry the man who got her pregnant. In Andrea's words, she was rape but according to her mother, the 22-year old man got Andrea drunk and "took advantage." The man was a friend of her sister and reportedly was either set up on a date with her or picked her up from basketball practice.

Known to her friends as "Drea," Andrea would divorce the man after over two volatile years of abuse but the union still produced two children. Armed with only a 9th grade education, Andrea had no skill set and bounced from job to job. She began working as secretary, waitress, escrow worker, model and touring exotic dancer.

CAROUSEL OF MEN

She married again in a union that lasted three days as her new husband didn't want her to bring her children into the marriage (she met him while setting a trap to find out who was stealing her morning newspaper.) Her third marriage was to a Jordanian national who needed a wife in order to stay in the U.S.

"I married for a third time to a young Jordanian student," she said. "He had cousins in countries that he was afraid he'd be forced to fight against. This touched my heart and I figured 'What's the big deal?'"

They divorced after a few years when the student decided to marry his own childhood sweetheart.

She married a fourth time to a "con man" named Dereck who introduced her to his gay lover.

At some point, Andrea did give birth to a third child but put the baby up for adoption in 1961.

ACTING CAREER

In her mid-20s, Andrea got a few acting gigs, landing parts in M*A*S*H, Bewitched and the Russ Meyer T&A classic Beyond the Valley of the Dolls. She would be credited under the name of Samantha

Scott but would also use pseudonyms of Donna Duzzit, Sarah Stunning, and Prudence Smythe.

"She had been a bit player in a lot of TV shows and movies," Riverside County prosecutor James Hawkins said. "She had some beautiful photographs of herself. Facial, bathing suit, different costumes. She was in plays, movies."

Andrea got roles in some late 1960s "nudie cuties" like Horny Hobo, Wild Gypsies, Nude Django and Bad Girls for the Boys. She did manage two get a two episode run as "Betty" in the show Bewitched which would be the high water mark for her in Hollywood.

"She really couldn't make it as an actress," crime author Diane Fanning said. "So she ended up working as a call girl to make money."

Andrea had been thrown off a horse while filming a b-movie. She injured her back and claimed that this forced her into prostitution.

HIGH-PRICED CALL GIRL & DRUGS

"I was finally dating!" she said recalling her decision to become a call-girl. "I had read all Harold Robbins' books to learn about men and a lot of my dreams did come true through with these 'pay dates.'"

According to her probation report, Andrea began using marijuana in her late twenties and used until 1980. She also indulged in barbiturates and morphine based pain medication after she injured her back in the fall of the horse. During her time as a call-girl, she would use cocaine.

MORE MEN

In March of 1980, she married another man after a whirlwind ten-day courtship. The marriage did not last two weeks as her husband went into a jealous rage. Andrea was able to fend him off with a butcher knife, chasing him out of their Los Angeles apartment.

"Andrea was an exceptionally beautiful woman," forensic psychologist Oscar Newsome said. "I mean absolutely beautiful. She knew how to use her body and looks and words to seduce men and get them to do things for her. She was in several relationships and marriages, all short and quick."

DESPERATION TIME

Now in her late 30s, Andrea knew her days as a high-priced call girl would be numbered. She had to meet a "sugar daddy" and fast.

Enter lumber magnate Robert Sand, who at 69 years old was 30 years Andrea's senior.

"Robert Sand had been a lumberman in the northeast," Hawkins said. "He made a fortune there. Retired to Los Angeles. He also had a long standing history with prostitutes."

Sand had been confined to a wheelchair for years. He suffered from multiple sclerosis and was confined to a wheelchair.

Sand had married his first wife Frances in 1939 but they would divorce in 1947. Five years later, they would remarry. She first found out about her husband's proclivities for prostitutes in 1973 which effectively ended their sexual relationship but not the marriage.

"His wife was divorcing him because he had an $800 a week prostitute habit," Fanning said. "And she was just not comfortable with that and she leaves him. So that's how Andrea comes in Bob Sands life."

By December of 1980, Sand had finalized his divorce with Frances. Then he began living with Andrea.

The rich businessman found the sexy former actress and model irresistible. He booked her for repeated engagements as Andrea gave him sex and massages.

"It got to the point where it got so expensive that his accountant recommended that he stopped spending money on her each month and marry her," Hawkins said. "To save money."

"There was the sizable age difference, of course," forensic psychologist Oscar Newsome said. "And the two were introduced by Andrea's 'madam'. So obviously we're not talking the ideal marriage here. It is an arrangement at best."

The madam informed Andrea that Sand sometimes "played rough" but treated the women he sent to her well "in general."

Andrea's fourth divorce became final in December of 1980 and she then moved into Sand's apartment in Westwood where he asked for her hand in marriage. Andrea said "yes" and they moved to a condo at The Springs in Rancho Mirage.

"They lived in a big, gorgeous home," Fanning said. "In a very wealthy area in Rancho Mirage."

"Rancho Mirage is where a lot of political figures, CEOs, and actress and actors retire," Hawkins said. "Its known as the playground of the presidents."

RESPECTABILITY

Sand provided Andrea what she always wanted, respectability and security. They had famous people in their neighborhood like Tammy Faye Baker. So in the beginning, Andrea enjoyed herself.

She wheeled Robert around in his wheelchair as he watched her play golf and tennis. He took her shopping and she would continue to give him therapeutic massages.

"She did have a power over men," Hawkins said. "She had a way about her. She was very sensual. And she would, for lack of a better term, suck you in."

"Andrea Claire was pushing 40 years old," Newsome said. "She had to have seen the writing on the wall when it came to her stripping and call girl days. She wanted the easy life. The rich life. So when she came across Robert Sand she put her best foot forward. Here was a guy, stuck in a wheelchair and had literally money to burn. Most importantly, she knew that he had multiple sclerosis which would only get worse as time went on. She saw him as an opportunity. Marry the old man, wait until he becomes invalid or dies off then enjoy the benefits of his wealth."

CONTROL FREAK

Robert limited Andrea's social life, however. He was a sexual voyeur and made Andrea pose nude for photograph sessions and walk around their condo naked.

"Robert was an old man confined in a wheelchair," Newsome said. "So like most men in that position, he did not want any kind of competition for Andrea. So he kept her confined to the house. They wouldn't go out to eat. He wouldn't let her out, period. She rebelled, of course, but he really want her to be his on-call sex toy."

According to Andrea, Robert liked to spank her with a paddle and masturbated while he watched her have sex with other men. Andrea claimed that Robert became more and more demanding with his requests and fantasies. Every day the envelope was pushed further and further.

"I think her life would drastically change due to a marital contract that we found," Hawkins said. "She agreed to perform sexual services for him. There was a whole list of them. Some of them somewhat perverted. And he would follow her around and photograph her doing everything."

Robert's demands would be increasingly kinky as the months wore on.

"According to Andrea," Fanning said. "Bob got more and more sexually demanding. And the sex that he wanted was more and more sadistic."

MUTUAL ABUSE?

Robert would have complaints of his own, however. He informed his attorney friend that Andrea would routinely berate and insult him as well as leave him alone for long periods as she went off to "play tennis" and that she had a "terrible temper."

"Sand would complain that Andrea would be abusive," Newsome said. "It is unclear whether or not she would initiate the fights with him or she was responding to his own increasing demands. What is clear is that he got more than he bargained for when he married her as he didn't expect her to fight back or display such a temper."

Robert Sand, however, was not going to throw away a Rolls Royce just because it had a few dents in it.

"But he was also compelled to stay with her because she had the most incredible body he'd ever seen," Hawkins said. "And the sex was wonderful."

POISON THE OLD MAN?

With the arrangement becoming more and more intolerable, Andrea contacted a friend and asked him about the effects of Seconal. She said she had already tried to poison Robert and that it didn't work. She also told her tennis partner that her husband would soon die from multiple sclerosis. Her friend said that multiple sclerosis would not kill her husband, Andrea said, "No. He knows he's going to die very soon."

"Andrea had been a sexual plaything all of her life since the age of 15," Newsome said. "She saw Sand as her only way out and yet this was not going to be as easy as she thought. She began to feel resentful at first then it turned into outright hatred. The sexual games that he made her play, paddle boarding, sadomasochism. For even the most hardened prostitute, it all became too much for her."

"That may have been the straw that broke the camel's back," Hawkins said.

Andrea had enough. She wanted a marriage of convenience from a rapidly dying old man. Instead, she got nightly sexual humiliations from wheelchair bound pervert who didn't want a wife. He wanted a sex slave.

"She thought it would be a life of luxury," Hawkins said. "Instead it was a life of somewhat sexual slavery and she just couldn't stand it anymore. Even though Mr. Sand was in a wheelchair I think he was a very demanding person and he exorcised control over her primarily financially."

THE ATTACK

One night in May of 1981 it all came to a head.

Bob Sand laid on the bed, screaming at Andrea to come into the room and perform her sexual duties.

Andrea, however, had something else in mind.

"That's when she attacked him with the knife," Fanning said.

"It was an out of control frenzy," Hawkins said. "Just stabbing over and over and over again. He was stabbed over 27 times and importantly he was stabbed in the heart and severed the aorta."

"The attack was 'overkill' as one psychiatrist at the time described it," Newsome said. "She stabbed the man over twenty-seven times so this was a hate-filled, raging attack of someone who had a high amount of pent-up anger. All the rage and frustration Andrea felt at the humiliation she suffered, hell, maybe all of the rage she suffered for her whole life bubbled to the surface the moment she started stabbing Robert. And she didn't stop there. She picked up a wooden board that she used for exercise and slammed it down on his head so hard that it caused a fracture."

On May 14th, 1981 at 4 o'clock in the morning, security guards at The Springs investigated an alarm coming from the Sands' address. They found the front door open and were soon greeted by an upset Andrea in a black robe. She told the guards that there was a male intruder in the home and he had run out of the sliding glass door in the living room.

She led the guards into the bedroom where they saw the bloodied, nude body of Robert Sand.

Forty-five minutes later, Sheriff's Detective Fred Lastar arrived and the scene was secured. Andrea repeated the story of the intruder and she was allowed to go visit a neighbor.

Investigators would later establish that Sand had been stabbed 27 times and had been hit over the head several times with a 1' x 4' exercise board. There was in fact a trail of blood from the bedroom to the living room's sliding glass door but they found only a single bloodstain on the patio.

There were no footprints on the grass where Andrea said the intruder escaped.

Lastar also found it odd that in the master bathroom above the toilet there was a wet-t-shirt poster of Andrea with her nipples visible under the thin material.

Andrea would tell the Sheriff that she had taken some sleeping pills and had gone to bed early the previous night. She had heard her husband screaming for help and when she investigated she saw one or two men running out of the house.

"She said she heard her husband yelling out," Hawkins said. "She went down the hallway to his bedroom, she saw some stranger in the dark who bumped into her, pushed her out of the way and ran out of the condominium. She went in there to find Robert on the ground."

She looked and saw that Robert was dead. Oddly, she went and washed her clothes when they had gotten bloodied after she tried to help her husband. Even more strangely, Andrea then went back to sleep for two hours before calling security.

"The problem with Andrea's plan was that not only was she a bad actress," Newsome said. "She was a lousy screenwriter. She came up with this half-cocked story of intruders breaking in and stabbing her husband. Sand is a well-to-do retiree. The intruder takes nothing and leaves the buxom actress all alone to sort things through. Right away, the Sheriffs doubted her story. She implored for them to go out looking for the intruder but they found no signs of forced entry. Nothing that would indicate that a stranger had entered their home for the sole purpose of killing a rich old man in a wheelchair."

No weapon was found in the condo but after a re-examination of the place the police found a four-inch kitchen knife under the couch. The autopsy would reveal that the knife was the murder weapon. When this was revealed to Andrea she went and "prayed" and then would declare that she took the knife out of Sand's chest. She claimed she washed both the knife and her clothes.

Laster then asked Andrea if she were willing to take a lie detector test and she refused. At this point, he considered her to be the prime suspect.

The attack on Sand was brutal. The autopsy revealed that the fatal wounds had been to his aorta. He displayed defensive wounds on his arms and wounds which meant that he had been conscious and trying to ward off the attack. The autopsy physician surmised that Sand had been lying down when the attack took place.

PSYCHOTHERAPY

Andrea consulted with her therapist, Dr. Morton Kurland, and he told her to stop talking to the police and get an attorney. He recommended Gary Scherotter, considered the best criminal attorney in Palm Springs.

Andrea heeded his advice despite the fact it was quickly looking like she was a black widow on the prowl for a rich husband to kill.

A TURN FOR THE BIZARRE

On July 23rd, the Indio Sheriff's department received an emergency call from Andrea Sand's residence.

When police arrived they found Andrea nude on the kitchen floor. Her hands and feet were tied behind her and a knife was stuck in her buttocks.

She told the police that she had returned home after a visit to New Jersey. She stated that two men and a woman had tied her up and repeatedly raped her.

During the rape, the intruders informed her that they had murdered her husband and would be back for more.

"The police came into her home," Fanning said. "She was bound hand and foot. And she had a knife sticking out of her buttocks."

"We never found any evidence of the assault," Hawkins said. "We couldn't find any physical evidence on her."

Detective Chris Brown realized that the rope had been tied with slipknots and there was the possibility that Andrea had tied herself up. During an interview with Andrea, Brown stated that he doubted Andrea's story.

"If you don't believe me, why don't you arrest me?" Andrea challenged.

"It's possible you'll be arrested," Brown said. "Based on my past experience, one of three things is going to happen. You'll either kill yourself, kill someone else, or I'll have another call back here for another phony situation."

MORE "ATTACKS"

Andrea began calling the sheriffs on a regular basis, stating that the same intruders came and raped her again.

"She continued to tell us that the intruders returned, kidnapped and sexually assaulted her repeatedly. There were so many incidents."

She also produced numerous threatening letters which she claimed were from the gang of murderers/rapists.

The letters were determined to be fakes as the only fingerprints on the paper belonged to Andrea herself.

"I've been on the bench for fifteen years," Hawkins said. "And I haven't seen any cases as bizarre as this one.

"In all of her alleged attacks," Newsome said. "Andrea was always the victim. There was never any physical evidence or signs of forced entry. These were phantom intruders. She was tested for DNA and they found nothing. So the police knew that they were dealing with someone who was either schizophrenic or making the lamest attempt to throw them off her trail. Amazing that she had so little foresight into what she was doing. Like a bad screenwriter, she had no one to bounce her bizarre ideas off of so she ended up doing a lot of bizarre things that only tightened the noose around her own neck."

FINDING A NEW MAN

True to the pattern of her life, Andrea could not go long without a new man by her side. She would meet Joe Mack Mims at a Christmas party at the Evangelical Free Church. Mims was 56 years old, widowed and a water pump consultant.

Andrea had a neighbor who encouraged her to "find Jesus" and she came into the church of Mims who was a regular attendee of the services there.

Mims became enamored with Andrea and believed her stories about the murder of her ex-husband and the repeated attacks. He went so far as to visit the Deputy D.A. Jim Hawkins and complained that if they knew anything about police work they "would probably have the murderer by now."

Mims then informed Hawkins that he was going to marry Andrea. Hawkins advised Mims against this, stating that they were going to charge her with the murder of Sand.

"Go ahead and charge her," Mims replied. "I'm still going to marry her."

"He became irate," Hawkins said. "He suggested that I spend my time trying to find the intruders that keep returning and assaulting her. And stop harassing her."

"Mims had a classic case of 'Captain Save-A-Ho,'" Newsome said. "Here was this woman who has worked as a call-girl, has two children, has been married five times and he is naïve enough to believe that after listening to a few sermons she is a changed woman. So he becomes her savior, marches down to the police station to intimidate them, marches down to the D. A's office. All the while, Andrea is not saying a word. She has a new man to do her bidding, to plead her case. She's damn good at finding these kind of men. She had been doing it her whole life."

FIRST DEGREE MURDER CHARGES

On March 25th, 1982, Andrea's attorney Gary Scherotter was notified by the D.A.'s office that Andrea would be charged with first degree murder. Scherotter sent her to the court where she posted $100,000 bail and was set free.

The next day, Andrea and Joe Mims were married.

SIXTH TIME IS A CHARM?

Andrea did not want to sell the condo at The Springs until Sand's estate was settled. Mims sold his own home and moved in with Andrea at The Springs.

"He took it upon himself to try and protect her from the return of the intruders who kept kidnapping and assaulting her," Hawkins said.

"Again, the poor guy is smitten by her charms," Newsome said. "Here is a 56-year old man living as an anonymous life as possible. He meets a woman sixteen years his junior. She's stunning, she's posed in Playboy, been in movies and now she is reformed at the church of his choice. He's convinced she's in love with him and is willing to move heaven and earth to make protect that illusion."

MORE BIZARRE STUNTS

Two months later after they were married, however, Mims called the police and informed them that Andrea had been kidnapped. The officers began a search but Andrea returned home on the same day claiming she had been abducted and raped by the same intruders as before.

No physical evidence was found but Mims remained steadfast in his belief that Andrea was telling the truth.

Andrea was able to put on a false front with Mims, appearing to genuinely care about the man as they would engage in social gatherings at church.

But on Halloween of 1982, Andrea convinced Mims that they should take a drive together. They drove along Highway 74 and turned into an isolated dirt road. Andrea threw a bed sheet on the gravel and began to give Mims fellatio.

Mims climaxed into her mouth after which she spit his semen into a tissue. She then told him to roll over on his stomach and she would give him a massage.

"So Joe thinks this is the best thing going," Fanning said

Mims was like putty under her expert hands but then something hit him hard on the back of the head.

He screamed in pain until he was hit again.

Turning around, he saw Andrea holding a hammer, wanting to hit him again. He pushed her off and grabbed her arm, ripping the hammer out of her grip.

"What in the name of God are you doing?" he asked.

"I've got to knock you out so that people will believe I've been raped."

Mims finally saw the light. He knew that she had thought to use the semen in the tissue to provide evidence she had been raped.

"The fact that she tried to kill him (Mims) was a real game changer," Hawkins said. "The evidence that we needed to really go forward on the case."

KNOCKED INTO COMING INTO HIS SENSES

Mims dressed and drove Andrea home before going to the hospital to get his head stitched up.

The next morning, Mims moved out of the condo. He notified authorities of the assault, prompting an attempted murder charge to be added to the first degree case against Andrea.

Mims moved to have his marriage with Andrea annulled. Andrea's bail was then revoked and she went to jail to await the trial.

Andrea's attorney, Gary Scherotter, now believed that she wasn't mentally stable and had the court examine her for competency. Andrea was taken to Riverside General Hospital for observation and tried to commit suicide twice during her stay there by slashing her wrists.

"Her whole world finally came crashing down," Newsome said. "She was completely out of control. A psychologically broken woman with no way out and no answers, she finally broke down and tried to end it all."

MENTALLY COMPETENT

Scherotter would resign as her attorney as the Sand estate had been tied up in litigation and she could no longer afford to pay him. Andrea was appointed a public defender in Charles Stafford who changed Andrea's please from not guilty to not guilty by reason of insanity. His defense lay in the hopes that the jury would believe that Andrea had been driven crazy by the men in her life who abused her and it all came to a blowout when Robert Sand forced her to be the victim in his bizarre, sadomasochistic fantasies.

But the prosecution found a man named Richard Cordine who was a convict serving a twelve year sentence for robbery at a Nevada State Prison. Cordine stated that Andrea had started a pen pal relationship with him in 1977 which continued for years until Joe Mims found out about it and stopped it. Cordine would testify that Andrea called him after the Sand murder and confessed "I stabbed the bastard."

Her prosecutor, Robert Dunn, would call her a "malingerer who would lie to achieve her own end." He dismissed the idea of Andrea killing Sand out of self-defense on the grounds that Robert was a paraplegic.

"She planned Sand's murder to get money from his will," Dunn said. "She received about $150,000 in cash and $100,000 equity in the couple's condominium."

"She stabbed the man twenty-seven times," Newsome said. "This scared the crap out of the jurors. Andrea would take the stand and give the performance of her life by recounting her tales of abuse but in the end, it was those twenty-seven stab wounds that stayed in the mind of the jurors."

After deliberation, a ten-woman, two man jury found Andrea Mims guilty of first degree murder. The judge sentenced her to 26 years to life and sent her to the California Institute for Women in Frontera.

"When the judge read the verdict to her," Fanning said. "She slammed down a box of tissues on the thing (table) and said 'I killed him because he called me a whore!'"

"Manipulation always worked for Andrea," Newsome said. "She knew how to manipulate men all her life. She thought she could manipulate everyone else the same way, cops, jurors, telling them about her tales of abuse and woe and thereby mitigating her own culpability in all the bad things she did.

REMARRIAGE?

Joe Mims tried to jump start his life after Andrea was sentenced but could not seem to get over her. He knew that she had killed Robert Sand but also believed she had been forced to do it as her attorney had claimed. He then heard a radio program discussing PMS and concluded that Andrea had suffered from the condition when she killed her husband and attacked him.

Mims did research on PMS then visited Andrea in prison, telling her of his findings. Andrea requested progesterone from the jailhouse doctor but the physician found no symptoms of PMS. He finally gave in to her demands, however, and the drug seemed to improve her demeanor.

Andrea displayed good behavior in prison. Mims had a renewed hope that he would get a new trial for Andrea on the basis of his PMS theory. He proposed marriage once again and Andrea accepted. He wrote love letters to Andrea such as the one below:

"My Darling Drea,

I promise you a love that will be true, I will always put you first in my life. I will do all I can to meet your every need, while we are apart it will be hard, but our God will bring you home to me. I love you with all my heart,

Your Hubby,

Joe"

On May 13th, 1986, Mims showed up at the prison to marry Andrea. He never made it past the front gate, however, as he began to experience chest pain then collapse. He was transported to to Chino Community Hospital where he was pronounced dead of a heart attack.

After Mims' death, Andrea once again reiterated her story that intruders had killed Robert Sand.

During her prison term she became a prolific artist at the Central California Women's facility and won several awards as well as becoming a Buddhist.

"I'm very proud of my achievements," she said in a prison newsletter. "I've used the past 20 plus years to improve myself, learning to grow in a positive way and also to heal and forgive myself."

Andrea was paroled in 2012 but suffered from ovarian cancer which soon got into her lungs. She would die at the Mesa Verde Convalescent Hospital in Costa Mesa, CA.

"I do understand that she suffered at the hands of men," Hawkins said. "Why she had the relationship problems that she did but I don't think that was ever an excuse to forgive or forget what she did to Robert Sand."

HUSBAND KILLER SHEILA DAVALLOO

NATHAN NIXON

Sheila Davalloo

Sheila Davalloo is truly one of the most demented individuals of the past twenty years. Several serious crimes are still being added to her gruesome resume. She portrayed the persona of a pleasant, happy person. She hid dark secrets, however, as to who she really was. The main victim was simply caught in a position that she could never escape from. To understand the vicious crime that Sheila Davalloo committed, it is important to understand the background of who she was. The totality of this murder is one that is still being uncovered. The lasting effects on an entire group of people has truly been catastrophic.

Sheila Davalloo was born on May 11, 1969 in Iran. She and her family immigrated to the United States in the mid-1970s. Like many other immigrants of the time, her family settled in New York in the town of Yorktown Heights. She obtained a great education while in the United States. She excelled in her classes and graduated near the top of her class. She was one of the most committed students in her school during her time there. Her family had really instilled a strong sense of pride in learning and continued education. She went on to go to college at SUNY Stony Brook on Long Island. This was a great location for her as it allowed her to stay close to home. Her family had a close bond and desired to have a strong relationship with Sheila. She went on to earn a degree in biochemistry in four years of schooling. This is an advanced degree and requires great dedication. This speaks to the mind of Sheila Davalloo and her ability to think logically and on a higher level than most.

Just after graduating college, she went on to start her life according to the "American Dream". She married her first husband, Farid Moussavi, in the year after her graduation. Farid was a close family friend that the Davalloo family had known for many years. He was a business man who had established a strong reputation in the area. Their marriage, however, would not last long. It is well understood that Sheila was never in love with Farid. This marriage went back to the culture of the Middle East of the time of family approved marriage. This was more of a marriage to appease the wants of her family. Her next step would lead her to cross paths with her gruesome reality.

Sheila Davalloo attended graduate program classes New York Medical School. She desired to apply her knowledge and move up to a bigger scale. It was at her graduate school class that she met a man named Paul Christos. Paul was an honest man. Sheila did not wear her wedding ring in most public places. Paul never had any idea that Sheila was married. After several months of friendly communication, the two started an affair on a grand scale. Sheila would frequently find excuses to come home later than normal from school. Paul was falling madly in love with Sheila, as she was him. Sheila knew that she could not divorce Farid, as it would be a disgrace to her family. After several months of sneaking around, Farid found out of Sheila's affair. He immediately filed for divorce and flushed her out of his life.

In 2000, Paul and Sheila married and moved into an upscale condominium. The location of the condo was 21 Foxwood Drive, Pleasantville, New York. The location of their residence would prove to be vital to the case.

Sheila seemed to be settled down in her new life. She was married to a man of her choosing, at her time. She had obtained a great job as a research scientist at Purdue Pharma in Stamford, Connecticut. This job was something that she had always wanted. She had always valued education and, to her family, this was the culmination of those efforts. However, something else would catch her attention at this new job.

Also working at Purdue Pharma was a man named Nelson Sessler. Sessler was a highly intelligent man. He was a lead scientist for the company and someone that had established a strong reputation of hard work, dedication, and integrity. When Sheila met Nelson Sessler, the two immediately hit it off. They were always working together and hanging out together on their breaks throughout the day. It was apparent to anyone that the two were flirting and very personal together. In a similar situation, Nelson Sessler had no idea that she was married.

Sheila Davalloo went to great lengths to protect her marriage and work from her affair. The lies she maintained and the stories she made her husband to believe were nothing short of strange and demented. Sheila became extremely enamored with Nelson. The pair had struck up a steamy affair that really had no limits. Sheila was desperate to establish a secondary life with Nelson Sessler. To do this, she convinced her husband Paul Christos to leave their house while still staying "happily" married. Davalloo told him that her schizophrenic brother would be staying over at their house. She named this brother Shahiem. Shahiem had no idea that she was living with anyone and would lose his sanity if he knew. At least, that is what Sheila told Paul. Paul didn't necessarily understand the odd request, but was happy to oblige to help his wife. Paul Christos packed up all of his belongings and moved in with his parents. This was odd to everyone around the situation.

Upon Paul leaving to his parent's house, Sheila Davalloo hid anything and everything that would give any indication that she was married. Shahiem obviously didn't exist. Shahiem was in all actuality Nelson Sessler. Sheila invited Sessler to stay over. Nelson was honestly a bit suspicious of the whole situation. Sheila convinced Nelson that she was divorced and happily single. While Nelson did not live with Sheila at this point, he spent many nights at Davalloo's home and they continued a steamy, one-sided affair.

Sheila was an educated woman who had progressed rapidly in her career. She understood human thinking at a high level, and understood that she had problem. At the beginning of 2002, she began to see a psychiatrist. She was still respectful of her marriage to a point that she didn't want to divorce Paul, however she admitted in September of 2002 that she always maintained a fantasy with Nelson. Her affair continued. Her communications with her psychiatrist would prove to be crucial after her crimes and would be used to find the true facts to her mindset in the case.

On Sunday, March 23, 2003, Sheila and Paul were spending a quiet afternoon relaxing at their home. Their marriage had been slowly pressing on, however their love life had almost screeched to an immediate halt. Sheila suggested that they play a game that she had learned at work. Sheila was becoming very flirtatious, so Paul was fully up to agree to the game. The pretext of the game, she described, was that he had to be handcuffed and blindfolded. Thinking this was going to turn into a romantic, kinky sex game, he readily agreed. Little did he know what was about to happen. Sheila lavishly blindfolded Paul and handcuffed his hands behind his back. Sheila was about to do the unthinkable.

Sheila Davalloo produced a 4 inch long paring knife from the kitchen. She violently stabbed her husband, Paul Christos, in the chest. The stabbing fully penetrated his chest, sinking the blade over 3 ½ inches into his chest cavity. Immediately, Paul panicked and begged her to stop. Sheila screamed out that it had been an accident. She was ever convincing and Paul was super naïve. He begged her to let him out of the handcuffs, however Sheila claimed that she lost the key to the handcuffs. Paul Christos lay there bleeding out, his life hanging by a thread and contingent on receiving medical attention.

Paul began to tell Sheila to call 911. Sheila left the room to call 911, and returned minutes later and told Paul that the line was busy. Paul was still handcuffed at this time. He had been stabbed in the heart, and was literally bleeding to death internally. Next, Sheila tried to get a doctor that was nearby to come to the house. She left the house for over ten minutes, but returned only to find Paul still alive. She told him that the doctor was closed. She the magically found the handcuff keys. She released Paul from the handcuffs and took the blindfold off of him. In her mind, she thought that he would be dead soon.

Sheila Davalloo loaded Paul into the back of her car. He was clinging to life, and seemed to be fading rapidly. She calmly and slowly drove to the hospital. Ironically enough, she didn't even go to the emergency room when she arrived at the hospital. Paul was begging her to hurry up. In Paul's mind, this was still an accident. He still believed that Sheila didn't mean to stab him with the knife. He would quickly learn the truth in a matter of minutes.

Upon arriving at the hospital, Sheila bypassed the emergency room entrance and instead parked the car at a secluded lot far towards the back of the hospital. She exited the front door of the car, and opened the back door. At approximately 5:30 P.M. Sheila stabbed her husband Paul Christos a third time, severely piercing his heart. This would be a near lethal wound. This time, however, there was a witness to the event. An onlooker from the Behavioral Health Center saw the confrontation taking place between Davalloo and Christos. The onlooker immediately called 911 to get help to the scene. Davalloo fled the scene and left Christos for dead in the back of her car. Davalloo was found by the authorities and quickly rushed into the emergency room. He was put to the top of the line and urgently taken into the operating room where he would undergo extensive open heart surgery.

The onlooker seeing the confrontation ultimately saved Paul Christos's life. Without the call, Sheila likely would have left him for dead in the back of that car and he would have been dead in minutes. Sheila also saved his life herself by taking him to the hospital. Hopeful that this would clear her name and prove it to be some sort of accident, she believed that he would not make it to the hospital. When he was still clinging to life upon their arrival there, she decided to stab him again to finish the job. Ultimately, the fact that he was so close to the hospital is the only way he managed to survive this brutal stabbing. Had this wound happened at their home, he likely wouldn't have even made it to the hospital alive.

In a further twist of irony in this already wildly bizarre case, Sheila Davalloo actually fled the scene AND CAME BACK! She fled the scene after stabbing Paul for the third time in her car. She came back to get Paul out of the hospital. She screamed at hospital personnel demanding they release him to her. Police were notified and rushed to catch her before she could escape. Unfortunately, she escaped out of the hospital. Police finally caught up with her. She was arrested by Mount Pleasant police. They took her to the primary jurisdiction, which was the Westchester Police Department. She was finally in custody. Paul was given a 50 percent chance to live through the recovery of the surgery. His body was in an extremely fragile state and his heart had been badly injured. While the surgery had successfully stopped the bleeding and fixed the apparent injuries, the trauma had taken quite a toll. Paul was left in intensive care to recover from his devastating attack. Police questioning would yield a strong sense of confusion and anger as they struggled to get any sort of truth from Sheila.

Police of the Westchester Police Department began their questioning of Sheila Davalloo that evening. She was questioned most literally all night. Police statements describe Sheila as being unwilling to vacate her story of it all being an accident. She initially explained that Paul's injuries were not even inflicted by her. Her story stated that his injuries were caused when he was working in New York City. This was an outlandish story obviously, however police investigated quickly to determine there was no truth to this. Nonetheless, police had enough evidence to hold her in jail with no bail set. This was crucial for the rest of the investigation.

Investigators needed to talk with Paul Christos to get his testimony. However, while he was recovering and looked as though he would survive the horrific incident, he was obviously in no condition to give credible information. Police needed his story, however they were forced to wait. Investigators looked to other sources to acquire more evidence and, perhaps, an explanation to this unbelievable act.

The police investigation team decided it would be a good idea to look at her cell phone records. Sheila had told investigators that she tried to call 911. She was adamant about this fact, being as how her story was based around a work incident that she tried to solve by taking Paul to the hospital. What police found was shocking. Police found out that she not only never called 911, she called someone by the name of "Nelson". This call took place at exactly 4:59 P.M. This means that she called "Nelson" during the stabbing. This was critical evidence to police.

Sheila Davalloo was vigorously questioned about "Nelson" and why this person would be called during the suspected accident timeframe. This was the only call she had made the entire time. Police found it suspicious that she not only lied about calling 911, but also that she only made a single phone call the entire time. Typically, when your husband has a catastrophic event such as this, or a workplace "accident" as she had suggested, then you would call some family to at least let them know what was going on. In such a dire situation, you would not load up the victim in the back of your car and park a quarter mile away from the emergency room entrance. While Sheila did not provide detail as to what was going on at this time or any sort of explanation, she did provide a solid piece of information. She declared to police that the man's last name was Sessler. This call was, in fact, to her lover Nelson Sessler. Police now had enough evidence to charge Sheila Davalloo. The following morning, she was officially charged with attempted murder in the first degree. Police now turned their attention to Nelson Sessler.

The following morning, March 26, 2003, Nelson Sessler was brought in for questioning in the case. Initially, he was believed to be a suspect. Police felt like he may have been an accomplice or "the help" within this heinous crime. Upon only a few minutes of questioning, police has informed Nelson Sessler that Davalloo was married to the victim, Paul Christos. Nelson Sessler genuinely had no idea. In all of the time they had been lovers, he had his suspicions, but none of them had been proven true. Sheila Davalloo had concealed this secret to him this entire time. Investigators asked him about the phone call that Sheila had made to him on the night of the stabbing. As grim as it is, he informed investigators that Sheila had asked him over for dinner that night around 8:30 P.M. This was a chilling declaration of the coldness of this crime. This also spoke to her true intentions with Paul; she wanted and expected to kill him. Nelson Sessler was cleared of any wrongdoing in the case. He was of no involvement in the crime, and Sheila herself agreed that he had not been at the house for weeks. This was the last piece of crucial evidence that police hoped would lead to the ultimate conviction of Sheila Davalloo for attempted murder of Paul Christos.

The final argument that the investigative team needed to make was a motive. To investigators, the motive became quite clear when looking back at the family history of Sheila as well as her previous marriage. To the Davalloo family, divorce was disgraceful. Sheila could not possibly divorce Paul and keep her spot in the family. She decided that if Paul had died, it would then make it respectable that she move on with her life. While this is a motive that could never be fully proven, police felt it offered the best explanation for the random attempted murder of her husband.

On February 4, 2004, Sheila Davalloo stood trial for attempted murder in the first degree for the stabbing of Paul Christos. The small courthouse in White Plains, New York was packed with people. This trial had drawn heavy regional attention and national attention as well. Paul Christos, now recovered from his near fatal experience, explained to the courtroom that he had never before seen Sheila act so violently. He went into great detail of how she showed no urgency to help him with what he initially thought was a sick accident. He explained that she left him to die, handcuffed and blindfolded, and showed no worry for the entire situation. Davalloo pleaded not guilty in what appeared to be an impossible situation for her. The opening statement of the prosecution is one that littered newspapers around New York and regionally around the United States. They portrayed Sheila as a deceitful, extremely manipulative woman who had the intelligence to violently get what she wanted. They explained that she didn't want to shame her family with another divorce, so killing rather than walking away was her solution to save the embarrassment. The overall goal of the killing would be to successfully and peacefully remain with Nelson Sessler. To wrap up their statement, the prosecution team played the interrogation where Sheila lied repeatedly as to how Paul got his stab wounds. The opening statement, for all intents and purposes, tilted the case in the prosecution's favor beyond a doubt.

After a relatively short trial, the jury was set to deliberate and decide the fate of Sheila Davalloo. On February 18, 2004, jury deliberations began. The next morning, they had reached their decision. Before he read the verdict, Judge Thomas Dickerson told Sheila a chilling statement:

"You tried to kill your husband. You waited for him to die, and have lied over and over again. You are ultimately a dangerous threat to society."

Davalloo was then read her conviction. She was found guilty on attempted murder in the first degree as well as assault with a deadly weapon in the first degree.

"She is a very dangerous woman who thought she would get away with what she did," Alison Carpenter, a lead investigator on the case said. "I found her to be deceptive from the beginning. She is very calculating."

Davalloo's parents chose not to attend the trial. They had been shamed and felt completely embarrassed of their daughter's actions. Sheila did, ironically, maintain a close relationship with her in-laws. She was seen sitting with them during the breaks of the trial in hallways and meeting rooms. Ironically still, when court officials handcuffed her, she told them to give her purse to her mother-in-law.

The relationship between Sheila and Paul after the trial was one that would be impossible to predict. While Paul ultimately filed for divorce from Sheila, he maintained that he didn't want her to serve an extreme amount of jail time. He felt that she suffered from a severe mental illness and wanted her to get help for that. Even after being stabbed to the brink of death by Sheila, Paul still supported her and wanted her to get help. This speaks volumes to the man that Paul Christos was, as well as the deep spell that Sheila was able to cast on those that were close to her.

The judge did not provide a bail amount for Sheila. She was ordered to stay at the Westchester County Jail until her sentencing. Paul and others pleaded for her to not get a severe punishment. The minimum sentence in the state of New York for these charges was 5 years. On April 6, 2004, the judge sentenced Sheila Davalloo to the maximum sentence of 25 years. She was given no possibility of parole for the duration of the sentence. This was devastating, but most within the investigation and follow-up of the crime felt that it was a fitting punishment to such a cold blooded attempt at murder.

If this story ended there, it would be considered tragic. However, it does not. She was also involved in a successfully completed murder. The details of this one are chilling and really show that the judge got the sentencing right.

Sheila Davalloo was convicted in 2012 for the murder of Anna Lisa Raymundo. The murder happened on November 8, 2002. This was just 4 months before her attempted murder of husband Paul Christos.

Davalloo was dating Nelson Sessler at the same time that Sessler was dating Anna Lisa Raymundo. All three of them worked at Purdue Pharma together. When Sessler became involved with Raymundo, he ended his relationship with Davalloo. This enraged Sheila and left her seeking a solution. On November 8, 2002, at precisely 12:29 P.M.

police received an anonymous phone call from a woman at a pay phone. The location of the phone was at a nearby restaurant on Shippan Avenue. This anonymous caller said that her neighbor was being viciously attacked by a large, light skinned male. Police went on to the condo to find the front door unlocked. When police opened the door, they were shocked to find the body of Anna Lisa Raymundo, lifeless and covered in blood, lying in the middle of the living room. The house was a mess. It was apparent to responders that there was a violent struggle that went on. Evidence to this included shattered glass all about, debris from all over the house, and blood spatters that were seemingly endless. High and low, it had all the look of a violent and heinous murder scene.

Autopsy records showed that Anna had been stabbed nearly 20 times. She had been severely beaten and had suffered a massive head trauma that likely knocked her unconscious. She also, mysteriously to police, had long hair in her hand. While this points to the struggle that police had suspected, it did not go with the initial figure that the anonymous caller had described.

In May of 2003, just 2 months after she was held for her attempted murder of Paul Christos, police announced that they were investigating a woman that Anna had worked with at Purdue. Since this announcement, evidence substantially mounted against one common person: Sheila Davalloo.

On November 6, 2007 Stamford police obtained a warrant to arrest Sheila Davalloo. Sheila was serving her sentence in New York for her attempted murder conviction. Police arrived at Bedford Hills Correctional Facility for Women where she was serving her 25 year sentence. They extradited her back to Connecticut to stand trial for the murder of Anna Lisa Raymundo on December 29, 2008.

Evidence against Sheila in this case was extensive. Most notably, security video shows her leaving Purdue Pharma shortly before 11 A.M. on the morning of the murder. DNA from bloodstains acquired at the scene matched both Sheila and Anna. The blood was found all over the house, but specifically a strong sample was found on two separate faucets around the house that show her efforts to clean the scene. The initial call that police received that day matches the voice of Sheila Davalloo. This was a chilling surprise in the case.

The extradition process for Sheila was not overly complicated. She agreed to be extradited to face trial for the murder of Anna Lisa Raymundo. She was initially tried on January 14, 2009 where she pleaded not guilty to the murder of Anna. After lengthy deliberation and a very odd trial, Sheila was ultimately found guilty of murdering Anna Lisa Raymundo and was sentenced to 50 years in a Connecticut State Prison.

Sheila still had to finish her initial sentence of 25 years, and then her 50 year sentence would start. She is set to be in jail until 2079. She will undoubtedly die in prison.

Sheila Davalloo has a story that is unique in that she naively believed that people would believe anything she said. This was held true by the lovers that she had in her life. The men that she was with all, undoubtedly, hung on to everything she said. She was able to carry on an affair for over 2 years without the other person even knowing that she was married. She convinced her husband, after stabbing him two times in the chest, that it was an accident. As crazy as this sounds, it is all fully true. The punishment that Sheila is currently serving is not near enough. Sheila Davalloo has proven to be one of the most vicious and naïve women of the past 20 years.

SERIAL KILLIN' SLUT : THE TRUE STORY OF SHARON KINNE

58

HEATHER FOX

"Sharon Kinney didn't want to be a normal average American woman. And crime gave that to her." - FBI profile Candice DeLong

Sharon Kinne committed two murders in 1960, shooting her husband James Kinne as well as Patricia Jones, wife of her lover.

Initially, Sharon was not charged with the death of James Kinne as she laid the blame on her two-year-old daughter whom she said "like to play with her daddy's guns."

She was later tried for the murder of Patricia Jones several times, however, with each case ending in a mistrial. Sharon would then escape to Mexico before a fourth trial could be held.

While in Mexico with yet another boyfriend, Sharon would kill a Mexican radio announcer named Francisco Ordonez. She would not escape the hand of justice this go around as she would be convicted in a Mexican court of law and be sentenced to ten years in jail. Three more years additional years were added onto her sentence after she unsuccessfully appealed.

But Sharon would never take defeat lying down. She would escape from the Mexican prison in December of 1969 and would remain at large to this very day.

This is her story.

CHAPTER ONE – A LIFE OF QUIET DESPERATION

Sharon Elizabeth Hall was born on November 30th, 1939 to Doris and Eugene Hall. She was born and raised in the town of Independence, Missouri with a brief departure to the state of Washington during her junior high school years. Sharon returned to Missouri at the age of fifteen where she attended William Chrisman High school. Her early years were relatively uneventful as her father did construction work. Her upbringing was middle class and Sharon displayed no outward signs of anti-social behavior.

During a Mormon church function in the summer of 1956, sixteen-year-old Sharon met twenty-two-year-old college student

James Kinne. The two would begin dating until Kinne returned to his studies at Brigham Young University that fall.

Sharon wanted to find a man who would take her away from the drudgery of Independence. The two engaged in pre-marital relations with Sharon seducing James out of his restrictive religious beliefs. She would letter write a letter to James while he was away at school and inform him that she was pregnant.

James would leave his studies at BYU and return to Independence where he would "do the right thing" and marry Sharon.

The couple married in October of 1956 but the marriage was doomed from the start. The couple really didn't love each other. James simply gave into his lust while Sharon used him for a way out of her mundane life at home.

The sixteen-year-old Sharon listed herself as eighteen on the marriage license and as a widow. When asked about her widowhood, she told people that she had been married briefly while she lived in Washington but her husband died in a car accident.

The couple would have two weddings with their second being a church affair at the Mormon Tabernacle after Sharon had converted to accommodate James' Mormon beliefs.

After tying the knot, the couple moved to Provo, Utah where James could continue his studies at Brigham Young. At the end of the fall semester, however, James quit school. He returned to Independence with Sharon and they both entered the workforce.

Sharon earned money by babysitting and working in small shops. James found work as an electrical engineer at Bendix Aviation.

Sharon would claim to miscarry their first child but she soon became pregnant. In 1957, the couple would welcome their first child, Danna, into the world.

The young couple would have another child but by March of 1960, their marriage was on the rocks. Sharon did not earn that much money and had to spend time at home taking care of the children. James was the sole breadwinner and found his checks being eaten up by Sharon's spending habits.

Sharon was twenty years old and already wanting more out of life than James could provide. He was a small town boy who said "aw, shucks" a lot and began grate on the young wife's nerves.

James tried to appease his beautiful young wife who felt entitled to the best in life. James would rent out a home next door to his parents and then built a ranch-style home in Independence. He worked the night shift at Bendix while Sharon would spend her days shopping and hanging out with other men.

"James fell victim to his the idealism of the times," forensic psychologist Tim Newton said. "He thought that if he gave Sharon all of the stuff she wanted then she would come around and give him the respect he deserved. What he didn't realize was Sharon was a different kind of woman, definitely not the 1950s June Cleaver type. She had her own moral code. And that code was to serve herself at the cost of everyone around her."

CHAPTER TWO – WANTS AND DESIRES

"I want a new Thunderbird!" Sharon repeated her demand as a mantra whenever James would come home after a long night's work.

"No."

"Aren't you tired, James? Tired of driving the same dull car every day. Those new Thunderbirds are soooo luxurious. We need to buy one."

"We don't have the money," James said, before trudging off to bed.

Sharon quickly grew bored with the marriage and the children. She would have another child named Troy but continue to carry on with other men.

John Boldizs was one of those men. A friend of Sharon since high school, he appealed to Sharon's carnal desires but not her financial wants.

"Sharon grew a hatred for the restrictive lifestyle of James," Morgan said. "She did not like the Mormon attitudes toward life and women in particular. So the marriage started deteriorating fast as James could not satiate any of Sharon's desires. No one could."

James began seeing the writing on the wall. He grew tired of Sharon's unpredictable shopping sprees and became suspicious that she was cheating on him

On March 18th, 1960, he had informed his parents that he wanted out of the marriage.

"She's okay with the divorce," James said. "But she wants to keep the house and Danna. She also wants a $1,000."

His parents, devout Mormons, convinced James to stick with the marriage.

"His parents were blinded to the dark side of Sharon," Morgan said. "They came from a mindset that a woman could do no wrong. They did not see that side of Sharon. She could be cold and calculating but somehow go onto the good side of people. You couldn't help but like her because you know that she didn't give a damn what you thought."

The idea of murdering James for profit began to percolate in Sharon's mind. She jokingly offered John Boldizs a thousand dollars cash if he could "kill her husband or find someone who would."

On March 19th, a day after James would tell his parents he wanted to divorce Sharon, police were called to the Kinne home.

Inside, they found James lying on the bed with a bullet in his forehead.

Sharon would report hearing a gunshot coming from the bedroom where James was sleeping. When she went inside, she claimed she found the two-and-a-half-year-old Danna on the bed next to her father.

The young child was holding one of James' guns, a 22 caliber semi-automatic pistol.

Sharon then called for an ambulance but they pronounced him dead on arrival at the hospital.

"My two-year-old daughter was playing with the gun," Sharon said, mascara tears streaking down her face. "It was loaded and when the gun discharged it hit James in the head."

Police were not able to recover any fingerprints from the pistol and a paraffin test (gunshot residue) was not given to either Danna or Sharon. Family and neighbors came forward and testified that James had often let Danna play with the guns.

Police noted that the young girl had a familiarity with the pistol that belied her age. The two-year-old had the ability to unlatch the safety lever and point the gun. Satisfied that the death was an accident, they did not file any charges.

The gun was remanded to the police as evidence and never returned to Sharon. She lobbied regularly to get the gun back but the authorities refused her request.

Sharon would collect his life insurance, a whopping $29,000 ($232,000 in 2016 dollars).

"Sharon Kinne was a sociopath," forensic psychologist Candice Delong said. "She had no guilt. No remorse about hurting anyone. She had no empathy for human life other than her own."

CHAPTER THREE – THUNDERBIRDS AND BOY TOYS

Walter Jones was married to a woman named Patricia and had two children with his high school sweetheart. A former Marine, he moved to Independence five years earlier. Patricia worked for the IRS while Walter sold cars.

Walter loved the ladies and immediately fell for Sharon the moment she stepped on his lot. With the insurance money in hand, Sharon finally had the opportunity to buy her dream car, a Ford Thunderbird. The two began an affair and Sharon looked upon the confident Walter as marriage material.

Sharon asked Walter to accompany her on a trip to Washington that May but the married man refused. She went on the trip anyway and when she returned, she used the same trick she used on James to get the man she wanted to commit.

"I'm pregnant," she said.

"What?" Walter asked, hearing her but not believing it.

"I'm pregnant," Sharon repeated. "And you're the father."

"We have to end this," Walter said, his face turning red.

"What?"

"You. Me. Us. It's over."

Sharon became enraged at Walter's attitude, fully expecting the car salesman to leave his wife for her.

"I told her to wait and see what happened," Walter testified at one of Sharon's trials. "I told her it was all over between us."

"Naked and screaming, Sharon followed Walter's car into the street, cursing and threatening to get even with him, as neighbors watched carrying-ons of a woman who had lost her husband less than three months earlier," a local newspaper reported.

The married car salesman had no idea the kind of psychopath Sharon was. Sharon would not let go and had to settle the score. She contacted Patricia at her IRS office of employment and informed her that Walter was having an affair with her sister. Sharon offered to meet Patricia at an undisclosed location where she meant to rat out the man that refused her hand in marriage.

Patricia would meet Sharon at the ended of a wooded street, a place known as a lover's lane for young romantics.

Sharon would pull a gun on Patricia and fire four shots in the form of a cross into the unsuspecting woman.

With his wife not returning home, Walter Jones filed a missing person report with the police the next day. He made frantic calls to neighbors and family asking if they had seen Patricia.

Her co-workers reported that Patricia had, in fact, received a call that day from an unknown woman who wanted to meet with her.

Patricia left work as usual with her carpool partners and asked to be dropped off on a street corner in Independence.

Patricia's car pool friends saw a woman waiting for her but did not recognize her as someone they knew.

His worst fears becoming realized, Walter called Sharon and asked if she had met with his wife. Sharon admitted to seeing Patricia and was going to tell her about their affair. Sharon went on to say that she saw Patricia talking to a man in a green 1957 Ford.

Walter became angry and went to Sharon's home.

The six-foot, two-hundred pound Marine was not to be trifled with. He held a knife to the Sharon's throat, threatening to cut her if she didn't tell him more.

Sharon talked her way out of the bad situation, convincing Walter that she did not know what happened to Patricia.

CHAPTER FOUR – DEAD WOMAN IN A DITCH

Sharon would call "Johnnie" Boldizs, her old standby boyfriend, and told him that she was worried that her friend was missing. She suggested they might find Patricia parked with someone on one of the many lover's lane roads around the town. Boldizs refused to "snoop" but agreed to accompany Sharon if they could visit one of the lover's lane themselves.

Ever the horn dog, Boldizs drove out with Sharon to their old make-out spot on Phelps Road in Independence, MO.

Getting out of the car, Sharon had "discovered" the body of Patricia in a wooded area.

"Let's get out of here and call the cops," Boldiz insisted.

"Well, take me home first," Sharon said. "Don't implicate me because I'm probably the last one who saw her alive."

Patricia had been shot four times with a .22 caliber pistol. She had a fatal wound to her head, the bullet had entered through her mouth on an upward trajectory. She also had a bullet that went through her stomach and two shots to her shoulders that came through on a downward trajectory. There were powder burns on the hemline of her skirt and police surmised that she had been killed at close rage.

"I was helping him look for his wife," Sharon said to the police. "He thought she was going out to meet another man. This street ends in a secluded lover's lane. We wanted to catch her in the act. Instead, we found her dead."

Police interrogated Sharon, Walter Jones, and James Bondizs. Jones and Boldizs both admitted to having sexual relations with Sharon and agreed to take lie detector tests which they both would pass. Sharon gave an oral statement but refused to sign a written statement or take a lie detector test.

Police had little luck obtaining evidence at the crime scene. They sifted the dirt trying to find the bullet that passed through Patricia's stomach. They employed a troop of Boy Scouts to help search for the gun in the area. This proved to be unsuccessful as did the dragging of a nearby body of water in the hopes of finding the weapon.

A .22 caliber rifle slug was found buried in the dirt where Jones' body had been discovered and police were satisfied that the killing had most likely taken place where the body was found.

Sharon would be arrested at her home for Patricia's murder a few days later. Jackson County Sheriffs also took the opportunity to arrest her for the death of James Kinne as well. She was later released on a $20,000 bond while she awaited her first hearing.

CHAPTER FIVE – COVERING HER TRACKS

Patricia Jones had been shot with a .22 caliber pistol and investigators discovered that Sharon had recently purchased the same type of gun. She convinced a male co-worker to purchase the gun for her but ordered him not to register the gun in her name.

Police searched her home for the gun in question and found nothing although they did find a box which they believed once contained the weapon.

"I lost that gun," Sharon said when questioned. "Lost it when I took a trip to Washington."

When interrogated about the gun later she stated that the weapon "just disappeared."

Her paramour Walter Jones did not get off Scott-free either. Police arrested him as a material witness in the case but he posted a $2,000 bond and was released.

Sharon would be arraigned on July 11th and was initially denied bail. She would eventually be freed on a $24,000 bond. At this time, she was three months pregnant and would give birth to a daughter named Maria Christine on January 16th, 1961.

Sharon would stand for the murder of Patricia in June of 1961. The all-male jury heard arguments which centered around cases built on differing times of death. The prosecution would state that Patricia had died more than 24 hours before Sharon found her body while the defense would claim the death occurred six to eight hours before.

The chief witness for the prosecution was Detective Harry Nesbitt who stated that Sharon had told him that she was afraid Walter was drifting away from her. She offered Walter financial support and tried to reel him in with the fact that she was pregnant with his child. The prosecution failed, however, in establishing the fact that Sharon owned or was in the possession of the gun that killed Patricia.

The jury deliberated for only ninety minutes. They found Sharon not guilty because of "just too many loopholes" with the prosecution's case.

Sharon had acquired celebrity status for the crime and one of the jurors, Ogden Stephens, asked Sharon for her autograph and she happily obliged.

But the police smelled blood. After she was acquitted, authorities immediately arrested her for the murder of her husband James.

They no longer believed that the two-year-old pulled the trigger during an "accident." Police hired a gun expert for the trial who testified that a child of that age would not have been able to pull the trigger on the gun that blew off James Kinne's head.

CHAPTER SIX – TRY AND TRY AGAIN

In the first trial for her husband's murder, the district attorney did not want the death penalty for Sharon. The prosecution also focused primarily on the testimony of Sharon's lover, John Boldizs. He would retract on his claim that Sharon offered him $1,000 to kill her husband.

"It was approximately two weeks to four weeks before Kinne's death," Boldizs said. "We was talking about her husband. She said, 'Would you kill my husband for $1,000?' I said, 'No. Hell no.' She said, 'Do you know of anybody that would?' I said 'Yes; I know somebody.' She said, 'If you find somebody, let me know.' I said, 'Yes.' But I never did."

"Do you have a feeling she was serious in her request?" the prosecutor asked.

"I believe so, now. She said 'Well, I'll just give you a grand. You can bump off my old man. Then I said, 'No, man. Like we wouldn't do that.'"

"Did you think it was a joke," Sharon's defense attorney asked, pressing the issue.

"It was just like if I'd say to you, 'I'd give you $100 to jump off city hall,'" Boldizs said.

Sharon's defense team immediately attacked the testimony of John Boldiz. "He was a poor mixed up kid who would sign anything," they argued. They also presented the argument that the young Danna had been able to pull triggers on toy guns with stiffer pulls than the .22 caliber used to kill her father.

The prosecuting attorney, J. Arnot Hill, remained steadfast in his closing argument as he believed that Sharon was truly serious about giving Boldizs a grand to kill her husband.

Sharon's defense attorney used their closing argument to soften the judgment of her promiscuous behavior. "It is not your role to judge her for being loose. What ever breach of the moral law, she has suffered and her God will chastise her. She has done plenty of penance for that."

The jury would deliberate for five and a half hours. They would convict Sharon of first-degree murder which Sharon met with stoic acceptance.

The judge sentenced her to life in prison at the Missouri Reformatory for Women.

Amazingly, James Kinne's family continued in their support of their murderous daughter-in-law, believing her to be innocent.

"We can't find it in our hearts to say anything bad about her," Kinne's parents said in a statement to the press. "We still don't feel that she committed murder."

"The verdict was a mistake," Sharon said afterward.

Her attorney's would eventually appeal to the Missouri Supreme Court which would reverse Sharon's convictions in March of 1963. They ordered a new trial because Sharon's defense had been denied peremptory challenges during jury selection.

Sharon would be denied bail initially but that decision would be overturned in July of 1963 as her brother would post $25,000 bond.

Sharon would then take her children and move in with her mother before the new trial began.

CHAPTER SEVEN – A BROKEN SYSTEM

Sharon's second trial would begin on March 23rd, 1964. The jury selection process would last over fourteen hours. Presiding judge Paul Carver had to sequester the jury due to the notoriety of the case. A mistrial would be declared when it was discovered that a law partner of the prosecuting attorney had once been retained by one of the jurors.

A third trial was then scheduled for June 29th, 1964. Once again, the jury selection process was a grueling one, lasting more than twelve hours. The testimony of her boyfriend John Boldiz remained the same, he once again stated that Sharon jokingly offered him $1,000 to kill her husband. But he further revealed that Sharon had told him not to tell police about the offer. A female acquaintance of Sharon took the stand this time around and testified that Sharon had joked that she should "get rid of your old man like I did."

The prosecution would reveal what later became known as the "Precious Tomcat" letters. These were letters that Sharon had written to her cell mate lover, Margaret Hopkins. Hopkins was an older woman she met in prison. Sharon had quickly learned the ropes in prison, obtaining an older lesbian lover for protection.

Sharon had entered into a handwritten "marriage contract" with Margaret during their time in prison together. Margaret would be released from jail prior to Sharon. In one of the letters, Sharon instructed Margaret to go to her grandmother's home and get the .22 caliber gun. The letter stated that the gun was hidden in a wall by the chimney.

"Lies!" Sharon would shot from her defense table. "All lies!"

Police would search the home of Sharon's grandmother but would later discover that she had moved. They ended up searching the wrong house.

No gun. No evidence.

Sharon would then take the stand on the last day of the trial. Looking somber yet elegant in a tight black dress, she addressed the all-male jury with her story of what place the night her husband James was killed.

"He had just cleaned his .22 and left it on the pillow beside him while he took a nap," Sharon said. "We were supposed to attend a church function and I was getting ready in the bathroom."

"Danna came into the bathroom trying to get me to play with her. She made several trips to the bedroom trying to get attention from James. She brought in several toys and asked him questions. Then I heard Danna in the bedroom. She was saying 'Show me this, Daddy. Show me this.' just as she had done several times before with her toys. And I heard a shot, I guess it was a shot. I went into the bedroom and Danna was standing there and James was lying there and I saw the blood and I thought he was dead. I picked up Danna and put her on the couch and called James's father."

She charmed enough of the all-male jury, deadlocking them seven-to-five in favor of acquittal.

This would result in a mistrial.

CHAPTER EIGHT – FOURTH TIME AIN'T NO CHARM

A fourth trial was scheduled for October 1964 but this go around Sharon would not put her life in the hands of the system. By this time, her mother had moved in with her and ran interference to

any authorities and press that came around.

Sharon then plotted her own escape. She became a barfly at the many low rent Mafia bars in her town, sleeping around with as many men as she could. It was in one of these bars that she met Sal Puglise, a petty thief and con artist. The two quickly became lovers and signed a handwritten "marriage contract" just like the one had signed with her cell-block lover, Margaret Hopkins.

Knowing that she would not be returning to Independence anytime soon, Sharon passed a series of bad checks around town. She didn't want to drop any more money than she had to.

In September of 1964, she was still free on bond. She took a vacation in Mexico with her new lover, Sal Puglise. She left her children with James Kinne's father while traveling under the name of "Jeanette Puglise", making as if she were Puglise's wife.

The couple had arrived in Mexico to get married. The terms of her bail permitted her to leave the country but the company that performed the bail required that she receive written permission from them in order to travel.

Sharon got around that loophole by using the fake name as she crossed the border. Sharon said she felt unsafe traveling in the foreign country and bought another gun in Mexico in addition to the one she had brought with her.

On the night of September 18th, 1964, Sharon left the hotel alone after an argument with Puglise. It is unclear whether she went to get money or get medication that she needed. Puglise would later claim that they were in their hotel room when Sharon complained of feeling faint. She wanted him to go out and get some medicine for her but he refused. Instead, she left by herself. She walked to the Del Prado Hotel but found the pharmacy closed. From there she went to a shady-looking hotel bar and asked for a drink of water.

An English speaking man offered to buy her a drink and she accepted. His name was Francisco Parades Ordonez. He was a Mexican-born American citizen who worked as a radio announcer in Chicago. He quickly became smitten with the beauty of Sharon and began plying her with drinks.

Sharon then stated that Ordonez invited her back to his room to show her some photographs and where she could rest as she claimed that she "wasn't feeling well."

"I lay down," Sharon recalled. "He took off his jacket and got me a glass of water. After a while, I started to feel better and told Mr. Paredes that I was leaving. He made some advances. When I pushed him away, he hit me and then put his knee on my stomach. He hit me several times. He covered my mouth so I could not scream, but I managed to throw him off and onto the floor. It gave me time to pull my gun from my purse. I fired — I don't know how many times; one or two."

Sharon insisted that she didn't want to kill or harm Ordonez. She only wanted to scare him but her bullets hit him in the chest, killing him.

The hotel manager, Enrique Martinez Rueda entered the room upon hearing the gunfire.

Bursting through the door, he saw Ordonez laying on the floor with two bullets in his chest.

Sharon stood over the dead man, smoking gun in hand, and then shot the hotel manager in the shoulder.

There are two competing stories as to what happened next. One story tells of Rueda having the presence of mind to run out of the room and lock Sharon inside. The other is Sharon getting into her car and heading for the gates but Rueda locked the gates in time and does not let her leave until the police arrive.

CHAPTER NINE – MEXICAN JUSTICE

The Mexican police believed that Sharon went out that evening to rob someone and had chosen Ordonez. When the man refused her demands, she shot him.

Mexican authorities searched Sharon's room at the Hotel Gin where they found two more guns and a supply of shells. They then searched through her purse, finding another gun and fifty bullets.

Her boyfriend, Puglise, would be taken into custody as well. They held him on the charge of entering Mexico illegally and carrying an unlicensed gun.

The couple would be held in separate prisons for their respective trials.

Puglise would be declared innocent of the charges brought against him and would be sent back to the United States.

But Sharon would find Mexican juries to be not as friendly as those in America.

"I just don't think about it," Sharon said before her sentencing for the Ordonez murder. "If I did I might be miserable, but I just refuse to look at things that way. I haven't given up hope and I don't think I ever will."

She remained resigned to the fact that she would receive some type of sentencing. "They (Mexican authorities) wouldn't feel they have done their duty unless they give me at least a few years in jail here."

Reporters commented that she seemed more worried about forfeiting a bond than the actual sentencing. "I could always use the money," Sharon said. "I don't intend to spend all my life in jail."

Her words later prove to be prophetic.

CHAPTER TEN – LA PISTOLERA

Authorities in Kansas would obtain the gun found in the couple's hotel room. Ballistic tests would reveal that the gun matched the weapon used to kill Patricia Jones in 1960. American authorities did not bother with extradition as they could not try Sharon again for the same crime.

The Mexican jury would find her guilty, however, and Sharon would be sentenced to ten years in prison. She again tried to appeal but that failed and resulted in three more years being added to her sentence.

Her fellow prisoners would refer to her as "La Pistolera" (female gunslinger) and the Mexican media followed suit, headlining their stories about her with that nickname.

Sharon would appeal as she did in the United States but her efforts would result in an increased sentence as the Mexican judge thought her initial sentencing to be "too lenient."

Now instead of serving ten years she was serving thirteen.

Sharon would remain in the Mexican prison system for over five years until December 7th, 1969. She would not present for a routine roll call at the Ixtapalapan jail. The prison guards were so slack that Sharon would not be declared an escapee until after she failed to show up at a second roll-call later that evening.

Her escape would not be reported to Mexican police until hours later as the jail staff tried to locate her on the prison grounds, believing she may be hiding somewhere.

A manhunt ensued and authorities focused on the northern region of Mexico. Investigators believed that Sharon could be heading toward the home of a former inmate that she befriended while in jail.

The FBI was alerted by Mexican authorities but agents did not think Sharon would attempt to return to the United States.

Multiple theories abound as to how she escaped and if she escaped at all. One theory is that Sharon bribed guards to look the other way while she made her escape out of the prison. A blackout had occurred the evening of her disappearance and it was later discovered that a door that should have been locked had been left unsecured. Another theory posited that Sharon used her feminine wiles to enlist the aid of a Mexico City policeman who was her boyfriend at the time. A more sinister theory speculates that the family of Francisco Parades Ordonez had helped her escape then promptly killed her.

The search for Sharon lasted only twelve days. Police believed that Sharon had crossed the border from Mexico into Guatemala which would negate their entire investigation.

Sharon was fluent in Spanish after the five years in the Mexican jail and could easily blend in no matter where she wound up.

By the end of December of 1969, Sharon was ostensibly a free woman with no law enforcement authority actively engaged in finding her whereabouts.

"That's quite a feat," Delong said. "And she pulled it off. That's the kind of person she was. Nothing could stand in her way. Not even prison."

To this day, Sharon Kinne has not been found.

IRISH BLACK WIDOW ANNIE MONAHAN

76

CARA DAVIDSON

Annie Monahan was arguably the most successful "black widow" of the early twentieth century when you factor in the time it took for authorities to finally catch up with her. She had killed three husbands and her own niece, garnering sizable payouts from life insurance companies as she acted as a beneficiary in all of the cases. She performed these acts of murder in the sleepy town of New Haven, Connecticut, dealing with police who always seem to be one step behind her.

Monahan grew bolder with each murder, increasing payout amounts in each case and even marrying the younger brother of a man she had killed.

LET THE GAMES BEGIN

Annie Pallman was a surprise guest at the party in New Haven, CT in 1906. She was dressed to the nines, with a brown lace top and her hair done up in a bun.

"The hell is she doing here?" asked Tabitha Long as she saw Annie enter through her door. Tabitha and the other guests knew that Annie had been recently widowed.

"She has the biggest smile of anyone here," Samantha Strong whispered to her friend as they both watched Annie make the rounds among the eligible men. "Jesus, at least, wait until your husband's body is warm."

Annie's first husband, Joseph Pallman, had died in November of that year. The coroner's had chalked up his death to "edema and pneumonia."

Annie herself benefited greatly from Pallman's demise, cashing in on a tidy sum of $400. She cashed the check and seemingly emboldened by the ease of which she had obtained the money, quickly put herself on the market for a new man.

"I think that during that time period it was relatively easy for a woman to cash in on her husband's demise," forensic psychologist Paula Orange said. "There was little in the way of investigation as long as she put on a false front that she was upset. The insurance investigators came, she shed a few crocodile tears for them and they went on their merry way, none the wiser that she was a damn killer. So I think that is where she realized that killing was easy and she became hooked on the power and adrenaline rush of ending someone's life."

The party she attended in New Haven that evening provided her with many a target. She soon e set her sights on a stocky Irish fellow with a confident demeanor.

Catching his eye, Annie would smile and turn away shyly whenever the man looked in her direction.

"Jackpot," the man whispered to himself as he straightened his tie and made sure his slicked-back red hair was in place.

"I'm Joseph," the handsome ruddy-faced fellow approached Annie as she poured herself a drink from the punch bowl. "Joseph Monahan."

"I'm Annie," the woman blushed.

The women around her continued to whisper, jealous that Annie had won the eye of the gregarious bachelor.

"Annie was not a politically correct woman of her time period," Orange said. "She didn't care what you thought, what the neighbors thought or even what the damn cat in the alley thought. She was going to do whatever the hell she felt like. She particularly did not care for other women, viewing them as competition. Sure, she was polite at first but if another woman got into the way of her and a potential target, watch out."

Nonetheless, she had a certain charm about her which enabled her to easily seduce the man she wanted.

"Most of the town gossips knew that Annie had been arrested on suspicion of murdering her first husband, Joseph Pallman," Orange said. "The police did not have enough evidence, however, and she was released. But when she made the rounds at local parties, women in attendance did a lot of whispering behind her back. The men were wary...until they got a good look at Annie and decided to take their chances."

Monahan was thirty-eight years old and physically attracted to the feisty Annie. He had never encountered a woman like Annie before. Annie was direct in her desire to make herself available to him. Most women at the party would offer token resistance.

But not Annie.

She invited the Monahan "back to her place" after the party adjourned. Raised Irish-Catholic, he felt it odd that the woman was being so direct and even more so when he realized that she was a fresh widow.

He expressed his misgivings, at first, feeling guilty about taking the place of her first husband so quickly after his death.

"It is too soon," Moynahan said as he began kissing Annie within hours of their first meeting. "Right? I mean, with your husband and all."

"He would want me to move on," she whispered into his ear. "Life is so short. We must not waste one more second!"

"Are you sure?"

Annie stepped forward, giving Joseph a deep and long kiss that he had only dreamed out but never experienced. "Life is too short, Joseph. Seize the day. Seize...everything."

The two made love that night. Joseph Monahan thought himself to be the luckiest man on earth as within weeks he had "found the woman of his dreams" and became married.

"I've always been unlucky in love," he announced to family and friends alike. "Now I am the luckiest man on earth!"

Little did Monahan know how unlucky he really was when he placed the wedding band on Annie's finger.

A BIRD IN THE HAND

"When Annie put her mind to something," Orange said. "She would stop at nothing to get it. Monahan was, simply put, putty in her hands. She brought him home and wined and dined him. Then she let the man try on her husband's clothes as if fitting him to be her next target."

Willing to ignore all of the warnings from the neighborhood, Joseph decided to proceed with the relationship with Annie. He introduced his new bride to his friends and family.

His younger brother, John, would also go into a trance-like state when he encountered Annie for the first time.

The young man stared in amazement at his new sister-in-law, barely stammering out a "hello".

"Come on, John," Joseph said. "Snap out of it."

"He told me you were beautiful," John said. "He didn't tell me you were this beautiful."

"Oh, you Monahan men are all like," Annie laughed, extending her hand to her new brother-in-law. "Charming and handsome."

"John will be joining us for dinner tonight."

"Splendid."

"Looking forward to getting to know you, John."

John nodded with shyness and took off his derby hat.

The young man had just returned from Army service. John was over a decade younger than Joseph and presented a more strapping, masculine look. Tight where Joseph was puffy, Annie now had her secondary target in place.

Annie began thinking, why be stuck with an old bird when you could have a young buck.

A year into the marriage with Joseph, her new husband began feeling "worn down." He soon found himself in bed, breaking out into fever sweats and writhing in pain.

The doctors arrived and could not confirm any kind of ailment. Joseph had always been in good health...until he married Annie

"Joseph suffered an agonizing death," Orange said. "She just watched him deteriorate each day."

Joseph would last until November 14th, 1909 as he eventually succumbed to "alcoholic gastritis", a diagnosis created by the doctors as they didn't know how else to categorize his illness.

Younger brother John was beside himself with grief. Annie played along, indulging in long and sympathetic talks with the younger brother way into the evening.

"There was nothing I could do," she sobbed onto John's shoulder.

"You did your best," John said.

"I should have done more," she wailed. "

"Don't do that to yourself," John said. "The Lord giveth and the Lord taketh. These things are out of our hands."

Annie would be questioned after Joseph's death as this now marked the second unexplained death in a row. The police and doctors believed that Joseph was the victim of arsenic poisoning but the symptoms weren't enough. They needed proof but Annie wouldn't provide them with the opportunity.

"He wanted to be embalmed," Annie tearfully informed the coroner as he came to pick up the body.

"Certainly," the coroner said.

Annie knew that she had to have the body embalmed before the police could order a post-mortem blood test. During this time period, arsenic was the main ingredient in the majority of embalming fluids. Because of this, police called off the autopsy as arsenic poisoning would now be impossible to prove.

The death now official, Annie was now free and clear of wrongdoing.

The life insurance company again paid her out $400.

"Annie was a smooth talker," Orange said. "She could ease over situations through charm and intimidation. Whatever the situation called for she was able to do. She could read which policeman would fall directly for her charm and play to their sympathies. With others, she would bulldoze through them in conversation until she got the desired result. She also did her homework. She let people believe that she was ignorant of certain things but she certainly knew her way around an autopsy."

THE REPLACEMENT HUSBAND

Two months after Joseph's death, Annie sowed the seeds of romance with her younger brother-in-law, John. In

January of 1910, the two would be married in an outdoor ceremony in New Haven, CT.

The priest marrying the couple would do something out of the ordinary. He break ceremony tradition and directed a question straight at Annie, the blushing bride.

"It has only been a month since your husband died," the priest said. "And this man has the same last name as your previous husband. Are they at all related?"

"Absolutely not," she sneered at the priest.

John looked at his bride to be, more than a little taken aback. She had just lied to the priest.

Would she lie to him?

"Annie was marrying her third husband," Orange said. "When she was suspected of killing her first husband and was currently under suspicion of killing her second one. You would think that young John would take a step back and say 'what a minute, what am I getting into here?' But such was the extent of her charm and power over men. John himself had very little experience with women. Here he was, fresh from the military service where he wasn't exactly knee-deep in women. Now along comes this super-sexy older woman who knows her way around the bedroom and his masculine psyche. In one way, you look at it and say 'how could he have been so stupid?' But, on the other hand, you look at the situation and realize how little of a chance he actually had once she put him in her seductive crosshairs."

The new marriage also forced Annie to take out a new life insurance policy.

Annie had badgered John daily to take out the policy (the magic number was still $400) and John himself began getting suspicious. Annie was still under suspicion for the death of his brother. The police and insurance investigators relented, putting Annie off the hook. This put John's mind at ease and he later takes out an insurance policy with Annie as the beneficiary.

"Again, these were the duty-bound men of the early twentieth century," Orange said. "It was considered noble and chivalrous to provide for your wife after death."

Annie would remain with John for over six years. It may be have been a case of her laying low after being suspected twice of murdering her previous spouses or it may have simply been a case of her enjoying the insurance proceeds. For whatever reason, Annie chose to remain with John longer than her two previous beaus but she eventually grew tired of him and eventually saw him as a liability to her freedom.

This discord would be exacerbated by the arrival of Annie's seventeen-year-old niece, Jennie McNamee. Jennie had moved in with Annie when her own parents died, her mother was Annie's older sister. Her youthful beauty easily eclipsed the now aging Annie. John could not help but notice the exuberance and beautiful blonde locks and Annie caught him glancing sideways at the young woman more than once.

"The roles were reversed now," Orange said. "Jenny was an absolute beauty. A knockout with long, blonde hair.

Annie realized that John may perceive her as an old bird. She immediately took stock of the situation and took action."

Annie would come along and watch the young Jennie play badminton outside with John who became Jennie's all-too-willing playmate.

"Jennie, why don't you go and clean out the kitchen?" Annie asked.

"The kitchen? I thought it was just the living room?"

"The kitchen and the living room. One of the stipulations of you living her is to earn your keep! Now you do what you're told or find somewhere else to live."

"Take it easy," John said but Annie shot him a dirty look for his intervention.

"The kitchen and the living room," Jennie said softly.

"Now," Annie said.

Jennie walked off in a huff.

"The girl just lost her parents," John said. "I know what it is like to lose someone."

"We let the girl slide and she won't be ready for the real world. She could work like the rest of us. She needs to find out that the world isn't having fun all day and night."

John shrugged his shoulders and dropped the badminton racket to the grass.

NIECE KILLER

Seeing Jennie's growing beauty as a tremendous threat, Annie put the sexy young woman in her cross-hairs.

Now familiar with the payouts of different insurers, Annie left no stone unturned when it came to her niece, Jennie.

Annie took out not one, but three different life insurance policies out on her young niece Each policy would provide over $800 each in the event of Jennie's death.

With the policies now fully secured, Jennie would fall ill during the winter of 1913. Doctors believed that it was mere "food poisoning" and instructed Annie to be sure that Jennie received plenty of rest.

Jennie herself didn't know what was wrong, complaining only of stomach pain.

Annie would remain at her bedside, praying with and encouraging Jennie, knowing all the while that she was responsible for the poisoning.

"Gastrointestinal issues in those days were invariably attributed to rotten food," Orange said. "The doctor seemed oblivious to Annie's own personal history. And that brings up another issue of those early times, the fact that doctors did not exchange notes to the degree that they did in modern times. Each doctor would come in blind, Jennie's doctor was ignorant of Annie's personal history with her first and second husband. Otherwise, he would have surely known what to look for and perhaps made a more educated effort to save the young woman. "

Jennie would lose the fight for her life on March 7th, 1913.

John took the loss particularly hard, growing quite fond of Jennie.

"Look at it this way," Annie said as the two looked down on the expired Jennie. "She's not suffering anymore. She doesn't have to suffer in this life or the next. Look at how peaceful she looks."

John said nothing, his mind processing the possibilities. Jennie, a victim of Annie's petty jealousies and need for profit. And who knew if he would be next.

DENIAL AIN'T A RIVER

Annie would "flatly deny" having anything to do with the girl's death even though she had been trying to collect on an insurance policy wherein she was the direct beneficiary.

The payout was delayed as the physicians could not definitively agree on the cause of Jennie's death. They found the entire circumstances surrounding her death to be perplexing. Jennie, a young and normal woman in the prime of life.

The insurance investigators now became suspicious.

They discovered that Annie had lied on the various insurance policy applications while a follow-up autopsy on the young Jennie would reveal "enough arsenic to kill three men."

Relatives would remember Annie sending Jennie's brother, Frank, to buy rat poison while his sister laid ill in bed.

They had Jennie's body exhumed and upon examination of the girl's viscera found considerable poison.

Detective Ward of the New Haven police department would arrest Annie on suspicion of murder.

"Remember that Annie was eight years older than John," Orange said. "She could bully the young man around with ease. So she easily got him to corroborate her stories of where she was and with who. It remains a travesty of justice that she got as far as she did. The lack of caring and investigative work given to the first two cases would have prevented Jennie's death."

The police then exhumed the bodies of Annie's prior husbands, Joseph Pallman and Joseph Monahan.

Annie, of course, remained one chess move ahead in the game.

"They were both embalmed," Annie said with a calm smugness. "They both wanted it that way. If you want to waste time, go ahead and exhume their remains."

"The police were at a standstill," Orange said. "She had covered her tracks well and they had no way they could prove that she gave Jennie the poison. The evidence was strictly circumstantial. A helluva coincidence, too fantastic to believe that she didn't kill Jennie yet they couldn't prove it. And she proved too tough under questioning."

The police decided not to prosecute after holding Annie for over nine months in prison. But the press went ahead and condemned her. Headlines blazed "Monahan responsible for deaths."

The local newspaper, the Morning Meridien, had a field day chronicling the history and circumstances for the "black widow" in New Haven, Connecticut.

John himself began to suspect, spitting out whatever coffee she served him and eyeballing his wife with suspicion.

"You believe I'm innocent, don't you John?"

John said nothing for a few minutes before shaking his head. "I don't know, Annie. I don't know."

"This isn't right," Annie said, looking at the newspaper report. "I don't even have time to grieve. Grieve the loss of my husband. Grieve the loss of my niece. They care only about sullying my good name and they have nothing. No evidence, no witnesses, no nothing."

"Only because you covered your tracks," John said, slamming his fist down on the kitchen table. "You know you're guilty. I know you're guilty. Everyone knows."

Annie reached over and slapped John across the face. He smiled, feeling the heat of the blow tingle across his face. He had finally stood up to her.

"Don't ever talk like that again," Annie said. "Ever."

John grabbed Annie by the arms.

"Don't you ever touch me again," he sneered. "Ever."

"The couple began to fight," Orange said. "Escalating into violent shouting matches. He would refer to Annie as a murderer, knowing that would get under her skin. He had no idea just how much he was getting under her skin or how much she would get under his."

Annie applied the same modus operandi as before, sprinkling arsenic over his food.

Her husband soon fell ill, complaining of stomach pain and weakness.

"That is the perplexing part," Orange said. "Why John stayed in the relationship. This could be akin to a man being addicted to his own abuser. We usually only think of those things in terms of how women keep going back to men who abuse them. But we don't think about how men do the same thing. Here was a woman who had killed his older brother, killed a young woman that he had designs on, then she commences to slap him around and order him to lie for her. If that is not a classic co-dependent relationship, I don't know what is. But in the case of John, his weakness cost him his own life."

Annie watched over the bed-ridden John for days on end. He would retch and writhe in pain, too weak to put up a fight. She would pray over him, feeding him soup that she laced with more poison.

Just as before, the family physician arrived and could not determine a cause of the illness. This doctor, however, brought in a colleague to help with a second opinion. This doctor knew of the allegations against Annie and he immediately transported John to a local hospital. The effort would be too little, too late as John would die in agony on June 12th of 1917.

"Before he was taken to the New Haven hospital," the coroner stated. "Monahan was so weakened that it was impossible to get an antemortem statement from him. The physicians who attended him at the hospital believe that he was poisoned. Professor Underhill of Yale will make chemical analysis or the stomach and other organs."

This time, however, the police moved in before Annie had a chance to have the body embalmed. They were tracking Annie and knew that she had purchased arsenic prior to John falling ill. They found traces of the poison in a vial taken from their medicine cabinet.

"The authorities were determined not to be outwitted by Annie this go around," Orange said. "They took out all of

John's organs and enlisted the aid of Yale Medical school to test for any poisons present."

An autopsy was performed and arsenic poison was deemed as the cause of death.

Newspapers described her as a "strong, featured, phlegmatic woman of forty years of age." She was held without bail after her third husband died in the hospital in New Haven.

"Monahan had been a semi-invalid for months," the doctor said. "He was killed either for his insurance or because he was a nuisance. So far we have uncovered but one policy upon his life, and this for the small sum of $250. But we have learned that an attempt was made recently to secure much larger policies from several companies."

The press would report that Annie would remain stoic throughout. She was informed that her entire home was searched and that they are "combing other cities in an effort to trace every sale of arsenic and other subtle poisons by drug stores."

"My husband died of natural causes," Annie said when questioned by the press. "The charges do not disturb me."

The press would have a field day with the allegations, labeling Annie as the "black widow of New Haven."

"Again, this was a time period that was hard pressed to believe that a woman of Annie's good looks and upbringing could be so evil," Orange said. "It wasn't until the death of her niece Jennie that the authorities were able to fully clamp down on what this woman was doing. It remains a head-scratcher as to why John remained with her all of those years. She was in jail for nine months of their relationship during which he should have left her. In his own mind, he probably could not bare the fact that both he and his brother could make the same mistake."

Two years later, Annie was brought to trial.

"I'm innocent!" she shouted at her trial. "You tried to get me every time. Every time you put me through this! I'm innocent!"

Annie entered her sentencing with a huge smile on her face after the jury found her guilty of murder in the second degree after deliberating for less than three hours.

She would be sentenced to life in prison and eventually die in jail.

"Annie fell in love with the control," Orange said. "Taking out those insurance policies gave her control. Using those bottles of arsenic gave her the power to access that control."

THE VALENTINES DAY MURDER

ANA BENSON

Richard and Stacy Schoeck had a perfect marriage, or at least it looked ideal for their friends and family. Even though they have been together for a long time, they seemed to have eyes only for each other. Richard was Stacy's fifth husband and everyone was certain that he was indeed the love of her life. The couple still went on dates and celebrated their love in every way possible. So when Valentine's Day in 2010 came around, the Schoecks were setting up a romantic little getaway and a card exchange in a picturesque Belton Bridge Park which is located in Lula, Georgia.

Lula is a quiet little tourist town so when their Police Department received a frantic phone call with Stacy on the other end of the line, they knew something serious had happened. The town was shocked to discover that a murder occurred right there in their calm little oasis. But soon enough, the sinister plot started to unravel and the law enforcement realized that things were not as they seemed.

So what made Stacy Schoeck turn on her loving husband and who helped her with the murderous plan?

Early life

Stacy Morgan was born in 1971 in Florida. Her childhood wasn't perfect at all and her father died when she was really young. This left a permanent mark on Stacy even though her mother remarried soon and she did have a father figure in her life. She was also molested during this time frame by an individual who remained anonymous to everyone around her. Stacy grew up to be a lovely teenage girl who would fall in love easily. She met her first husband while she was still in high school and the couple got married shortly after. Unfortunately, he wasn't what Stacy was looking for and it took her two years to come to this conclusion. She filed for a divorce and the two separated.

When Stacy was twenty years old, she met her second husband. Soon after the wedding, Stacy found out that she was pregnant with her first child. The marriage lasted a little more than a year and she once again filed for a divorce when her son was just a toddler. Instead of being beaten down by two failed marriages, Stacy remained strong and made a decision to improve herself. After all, she was only twenty-two years old. She applied for college and got accepted. Stacy moved on to raise her son on her own and earn a degree in psychology and nursing at the same time.

She managed to find the employment as soon as she got out of college. Stacy was still very optimistic about her love life and wanted to find someone to spend the rest of her life with. She met her third husband in 1997 but unfortunately, the marriage was short-lived once again. It lasted for only six weeks. Stacy decided to date casually in the future and gave birth to her second son in 1998. She was still a single mother but this didn't seem to bother her at all.

Stacy did need to improve her financial status and she found a better job opportunity at a clinic which was located in Atlanta. The family moved over there and she was ready to start over. She got an excellent position at the hospital's administration with the possibility of even better promotion. She would assist the doctors on a daily basis with various tasks. Stacy was a successful and independent woman who was capable of taking care of her two small boys on her own.

But something was still missing and Stacy was longing for a partner who would be there for her. She was tired of casual encounters and needed some stability. So in 2001 she married for the fourth time and moved out to a small town near Atlanta. She got pregnant once again and gave birth to her third son. She lived in a large house with her fourth husband and it seemed that her life was absolutely perfect. Her boys were happy and they loved the suburban lifestyle. On the other hand, Stacy was still unhappy. Soon after the separation from her fourth husband in 2005, Stacy met Richard Schoeck, a graphic designer who was slightly older than her. He was a patient at the hospital where Stacy worked at the time. The two hit it off immediately.

Richard Schoeck was an adventurer who lived his life to the maximum. Stacy was immediately attracted to his positive attitude and passionate outlook. Richard accepted Stacy's sons like they were his own and would often organize family outings that included the entire family. She loved how different Richard was from all of her previous husbands and thought that she had finally found the one.

Unconcerned about Stacy's previous failed marriages, Richard still wanted to make their relationship permanent. The couple did get married in 2007 but the ceremony wasn't standard at all. Stacy and Richard eloped and told everyone about the wedding once they came back home. It was in Richard's nature to do something so spontaneous and Stacy adored him for that.

Richard became a stay at home dad after the wedding and he would form a close bond with Stacy's boys. He was very involved with their school and hobbies so he ended up adopting the youngest two. He really did accept this small family as his own and wanted the best for the boys. Everyone approved of Richard and Stacy's family hoped that she finally found the man of her life. Unfortunately, this marriage would end up tragically in just a couple of years.

The murder of Richard Schoeck

Prior to Valentine's Day in February of 2010, Stacy invited Richard on a small romantic getaway to the town of Lulu, Georgia. They were supposed to meet in Belton Bridge Park which is a secluded area near the town itself and exchange gifts there. This wasn't unusual for the Schoecks because they would often go on different adventures that were supposed to spice up their love life. The Police dispatchers received a frantic phone call sometime after the nightfall. Stacy was screaming that her husband was shot and robbed. He wasn't showing any signs of life.

The police arrived at the scene of the crime and sure enough, Richard's body was lying next to his pickup truck. The blood was both inside and outside of the vehicle which meant that several shots were fired. At least one bullet hit him while he was still in the driver's seat or getting out of the car. He crawled out, perhaps to run away or defend himself. The shooter continued firing the gun until they were certain that Richard was dead.

The investigators immediately closed off the area and examined the tire tracks which were visible in the surrounding mud. They noticed that the third vehicle was definitely there and that it left the scene of the crime prior to the arrival of Stacy. The law enforcement marked them as the evidence. However, there were some red flags that indicated that this wasn't a standard robbery. For instance, Richard's valet was still in the car and his jewelry was on him. Nothing was taken from the scene.

Stacy wasn't a suspect at the time but the police escorted her to the station in order to interview her and get as many details as possible. Lulu is a quiet town where crime rarely happens so the law enforcement couldn't zero in on any possible reason why Richard was shot. One theory suggested that he might have interrupted another couple at Belton Bridge Park because it was a common meeting ground for lovebirds who wanted to spend some time together outside of their homes.

The interviews and investigation

Once Stacy got to the station, she started talking. She was asked to explain what they were doing at the remote park and she admitted that they did have problems in their marriage. She thought this would be the perfect time to add some flare to their relationship. Since Richard was a stay at home dad and she had difficult work hours, the two simply couldn't get any alone time to spend with each other. She was becoming desperate and unhappy.

She quickly admitted to having an affair to the shock of everyone who was present in the interrogation room. Her lover was a fellow co-worker from the hospital who was significantly younger than Richard. His name was Juan and he was a complete opposite of Stacy's husband. She needed intimacy and she fell in love with someone else who could give her everything she craved for. Stacy even took her lover to Las Vegas just a couple of weeks prior to the murder of her husband.

The detectives were interested in the affair and started asking questions related to the possibility that Stacy wanted to get out of her marriage with Richard in order to be with her new man. Stacy told them that she did think about leaving Richard but that no particular plans were made. She knew how much her children loved him and getting a divorce would probably break their hearts. They focused on Stacy's lover but she quickly debunked their claims by saying that he is not violent at all and that she cannot imagine him being involved with anything involving guns or shooting.

But Stacy did say that Juan knew about the rendezvous in the park so the police decided to call him up for an interview the next morning. Juan seemed oblivious to the events that took place last night and he told the detectives that Stacy claimed her relationship with Richard was open. This meant that each of them had someone on the side. Juan didn't seem to be bothered by this arrangement at all so the investigators started doubting their possible theory. Plus, Juan had a solid alibi for the time of the murder because he was in another city.

They were left without any solid lead in this case so it was time to look a bit further and include as much aid as possible. The park is a fairly isolated place but there was a nearby cell phone tower that covered the entire area. The investigators knew that if a call was placed from that location on the night of the murder, they would have the number listed. And it turned out that this was a crucial move made by the investigators because it would lead them in the right direction.

The list of calls was short because that cell tower is not in an urban area. The detectives used the contact information which was stored in both Stacy's and Richard's phones and they tried to find the match. Stacy's phone had the number that was called sometime around the murder. The contact info itself stood out because it said Mr. Results. The investigators were slightly confused because they had no idea who this person was. But calling him up would probably shed some light on the events that occurred on Valentine's Day.

The police quickly identified the mystery man who was present at the scene of the crime that night. His name was Reginald Coleman and he worked as a private fitness instructor in Atlanta. Coleman was born in Philadelphia but his criminal past led him to move out from his hometown and try to start over in another state. He was incarcerated in the past but managed to clean up his act. Coleman was doing fine financially and owned a fairly popular gym. As far as the local police force knew, he was staying away from any type of crime.

Todd Woodten who would become Coleman's attorney during the trial said the following on his client: "Reginald was a true survivor. He was street-savvy and always had a hustle going on. He did a lot of things for youth, trying to keep them off the street and keep them safe."

Once the police managed to attain the call records from Reginald Coleman's cell phone, they found the number he had called from the Belton Bridge Park. The investigators thought they would see Stacy Schoeck's digits but they were surprised with their discovery. Coleman called another woman - Lynitra Ross. The detectives then realized that the whole plot was more complicated that they initially assumed and that there are more players involved with the murder of Richard Schoeck. So how did all of them fit together?

After speaking to Coleman's friends, the police found out that Lynitra Ross was his ex-girlfriend who would often resurface in his life. But there was another detail that connected Lynitra to the murder – she worked at the same hospital as Stacy Schoeck and two of them were really good friends. Stacy was Lynitra's boss and a landlord. Since there was a third set of tire marks on the scene of the murder, the detectives quickly determined that the model did not fit the tires on Reginald's car. This did sidetrack them a bit but they were still determined to find out what really happened.

The investigators were certain that they did, in fact, have their suspect and that was Stacy Schoeck. However, they still had to connect the dots so they dug even further into the phone records of those three. There was a message exchange on the night prior to the murder of Richard Schoeck between the three parties. However, the most interesting clue was Stacy's bank account which clearly stated that she sent a total of $10,000 to Lynitra's account which she passed along to Reginald.

The arrests

Since the topic of the third vehicle was still the big unknown, the police started going through all cars which were somehow related to Stacy, Lynitra, and Reginald. And soon enough they were onto something. Stacy did have one car which she sold soon after the murder. It wasn't registered to her but she did use it often in order to drive her relatives or get them groceries. They were surprised to find out that Stacy put their vehicle on the market but she told them that they will get a newer model as a gift from her.

The police became very suspicious of this story so they tracked down the new owner and took a look at the tires as well as the insides of the car. And yes, the tire marks matched perfectly. Stacy Schoeck borrowed that car to Reginald Coleman on that fatal Valentine's Day. The evidence against Coleman was piling up and he was arrested on May 25th, 2010. But as soon as the interrogation started, he denied any involvement with Stacy Schoeck or the murder of her husband.

Lynitra Ross was arrested a couple of hours after Reginald but she also refused to provide the investigators with any useful information. It was time to pick up Stacy as well so the police arrived at the medical center she worked at and led her straight to the station. The investigators had plenty of circumstantial evidence to accuse her of the murder and they didn't have to wait for her accomplices to start talking about the crime. All three of them were in custody and it was time to face the justice for their actions.

Psychological assessment

Stacy Schoeck was put through a psychological assessment prior to the trial itself in order to determine if she had any underlying problems which were unknown to her or her family. The murder was well planned so she clearly wasn't distraught at the time which meant that Stacy knew exactly what she was doing when she asked her friend Lynitra to help her get rid of her husband.

The psychologists took a closer look at her prior relationships and marriages which ended in divorce. The reason for her unhappiness might lay in the fact that she lost her biological father when she was young and she was unable to connect to anyone. Not to forget that Stacy was also molested when she was just a child.

It was obvious that Stacy Schoeck was manipulative and knew how to get exactly what she wanted in every situation. Her intelligence was obviously high because she did put herself through school and successfully earned her degrees. However, her actions towards Richard Schoeck show that Stacy was also a sociopath because she hired a man to murder her husband and continued to live her life as nothing happened.

She mourned her husband publicly and got very emotional in front of her friends and family every time they saw her. The fact that she selected Valentine's Day as the date of the execution speaks volumes about her cold-heartedness towards Richard Schoeck.

The trials of Ross and Coleman

The first of three to stand a trial was Lynitra Ross. She entered the courtroom in May 2012 and was facing charges for a murder. After all, she was a co-conspirator who helped Stacy Schoeck find the hitman who would eventually pull the trigger and take Richard's life. Stacy was also present in the courtroom but she wasn't the accused in this situation. As a matter of fact, she testified on the side of the prosecution.

Stacy Schoeck was cooperating with the law enforcement and made a deal regarding her sentencing. She did everything to avoid the death penalty and was ready to talk about the murder of her husband. It was clear that her deeds were out in the open and she said the following as she took the stand: "I'm going to testify truthfully for Richard. It's all I can give his mom and his family and the children — all I can give them is the truth."

The jury then heard the story about the murder plot. Stacy Schoeck had the idea to take her husband's life in December 2009 after she noticed that her boys were acting strangely. They were getting into troubles and she started to suspect that they might be victims of molestation. She remembered how she behaved during the time she was assaulted as a child and found the connection. Of course, her first suspect was Richard because he was always with the boys.

Stacy also said: "I was just so fixated in my mind that Richard was doing something wrong that I said, 'I don't want the cops, I don't want a divorce, I want him dead.'" She then admitted to asking an unnamed man to help her kill her husband but he stopped returning her calls. Then she talked to her friend and co-worker Lynitra Ross and told her about her suspicions. Lynitra responded with the suggestion that they talk to her ex-boyfriend who would know what to do because he was "an experienced hitman".

After Lynitra Ross contacted Coleman, the two woman drove to his house and sat down with him in order to agree on some finer details regarding the hit. They talked and ate food from Zaxby's. Stacy suggested the park as the perfect place for executing her husband because he wouldn't suspect a thing. Reginald and Stacy agreed on the amount of money she would pay him for the murder, as well as on the vehicle he would take to the park. All three of them went to Belton Bridge Park so that Stacy could show him the exact place where her husband will be waiting.

Stacy noted in her testimony the following: "The only times I ever saw or spoke to Reginald Coleman was the day we had Zaxby's that afternoon and the following Saturday when we went up to Belton

Bridge. Everything else was done through Lynitra." She also added that she had given Lynitra the property she was renting to her as the payment for the help.

Lynitra's defense lawyers took the stand and told the jury that Stacy's testimony which involved the molestation claims was slightly off due to the fact that she admitted to having an affair in the first interview she gave after the murder. She didn't mention anything related to the possible sexual abuse of her children.

In August of 2012, Lynitra Ross was sentenced to life in prison. There would be no possibility of a parole either. Even though she didn't pull the trigger, she was the person who set up Stacy and Reginald to meet. Therefore, she was directly involved in the murder plot.

It was later determined that Richard Schoeck didn't have anything to do with child molestation but Stacy's plan was already completed and her husband was dead. The investigators took her claims seriously and talked to the middle boy who immediately said that he never accused Richard of anything. As a matter of fact, he never even talked to his mother about the alleged abuse. However, this didn't stop Stacy's attorneys from building their case around this.

Reginald Coleman's trial didn't last long because as soon as he appeared in front of the judge in November of 2012, he pleaded guilty to the murder of Richard Schoeck. He also faced charges for owning the firearm as a convicted felon. Stacy Schoeck was set to testify against him as well, which meant providing the courtroom with the full account of Reginald's actions.

Reginald Coleman agreed to kill Richard Schoeck after he heard the story of the alleged molestation directly from Stacy and Lynitra. Since he grew up in foster care, he often listened to the stories from his friends about their own abuse. Coleman thought that he could help the boys have a normal childhood by eliminating the threat from their life. He pleaded guilty in order to avoid the death penalty which was already on the table if he went on a trial. Coleman received the punishment of life in prison without the possibility of a parole and some additional years for the possession of the firearm.

Stacy Schoeck's trial

Once Ross and Coleman received their sentences, it was time for Stacy to appear in court for her own trial. The proceedings began in December of 2012 at Hall County Courtroom. Since Stacy cooperated with the prosecution in the trials of Coleman and Ross, the death penalty was off the table. Judge Jason Deal listened to the witnesses who described Richard Schoeck as a loving father and an exceptional friend who would never harm anyone. Stacy's defense attorneys once again repeated the story of the alleged abuse and claimed that her actions were severe because she wanted to protect her children from the aggressor.

When Stacy took the stand, she admitted to the crime and asked the judge to give her mercy. The defense told the courtroom about Stacy's own abuse and that she was acting erratically. However, the fact that the murder was planned months before it happened painted a picture of someone who wanted to eliminate her husband. Stacy had plenty of time to make sure that Richard was really the abuser and contact the law enforcement but she failed to do so.

Stacy's lawyers asked Judge Deal to consider giving Stacy a possibility of a parole and to keep in mind her troubled past. They also pointed out that Stacy was behaving well in prison and that she deserves a second chance. However, she received the punishment of life in prison without a chance to get out after serving thirty years which was the primary goal of her defense team.

Attorney Lee Darragh who led the prosecution said: "Judge Jason Deal appropriately recognized that Stacey Schoeck was the engine that put this train in motion, until the death of her husband. Without her involvement, this would not have occurred." The courtroom was filled with emotions because a large number of Richard's friends showed up for the hearing. One of the saddest moments was when Stacy's mother read a note which was written by her youngest boy which said: "I miss her every hour of every day, just like Daddy Richard."

Initially, Stacy Schoeck and Lynitra Ross were placed in two separate prisons in order to avoid any possible conflicts between the two but they were soon moved to the same facility – Pulaski State Prison. Stacy's family was left to wonder what was really the reason for this heinous crime because the exact motive was never uncovered. They got the custody of Stacy's three sons.

BARBARA STAGER :

A BLACK WIDOW

108

SAMANTHA REED

Barbara Stager: A Black Widow

There are many stories of black widows, women who kill their husbands for power or financial gain. These women have been scattered throughout history and the ones who have been caught for their crimes often make us take a second to consider what the people we love, and believe love us, are truly capable of. You may never know whom you are sleeping next to, but should you really be concerned that they will poison your oatmeal or shoot you while you sleep? It's a rare occurrence, but it does happen.

One such case comes from the sleepy city of Durham, North Carolina. Durham was a tight knit town, a wholesome community where people were proud to raise their children, work, and attend their churches. And even decades later, the residences of Durham have not forgotten what happened when evil walked through their town.

In The Beginning

Barbara Ford, born Barbara Terry in 1948, is an average American woman to everyone who meets her. She has been happily married for almost ten years. She is a devout Christian and member of the community. She is a mother of two sons, Brian and Jason, both of which she loves deeply and she is an attentive wife.

No one questioned her story when her husband Larry Ford died, tragically according to Barbara, in an accidental shooting. While cleaning his firearm, a 25-caliber pistol, Larry accidentally shot himself in the chest and died from the injury. The police ruled this a suicide at first and then later changed their decision to an accidental shooting.

The whole town of High Point, North Carolina, where Barbara and Larry had called home with their two children, agreed that this was tragic but that there was nothing suspicious about it. The only ones to question what had happened to Larry were his family. They seemed to believe that there was no way Larry would "accidentally" shoot himself. Their suspicion fell on deaf ears, at the time, and they were left to wonder what had actually happened.

Meanwhile, Barbara Ford packed up her belongings and her two sons and moved back home to Durham, North Carolina, her hometown, to stay with her parents. To all appearances she was seeking solace from the loss of her first husband with family and attempting to rebuild a life for herself and her sons.

It took her very little time to find this new life.

Barbara settled into a new house in Durham with her two sons, a house that was just down the road from Russell Stager. Russell, or Russ to anyone who knew him, was currently going through a divorce from his first wife, Jo Lynn Snow, whom he had been married to for just under four years. High school sweethearts at the time, they found that life was taking them in different directions and despite the divorce they remained good friends.

Russ and Barbara hit things off rather immediately. The chemistry between the two was rather evident even if friends of Russ could not see why he was particularly drawn to her. Barbara inserted herself rather fully into his life and rather quickly after meeting him. They were inseparable. She attended the sporting events that he coached and participated in. She was openly affectionate with him. It was not difficult to see where things were going with the couple.

They were engaged in a few short months and before the ink had even dried on his divorce papers they were married.

A Happy Couple

Russ Stager was an upstanding member of the community. He was a high school gym teacher, he coached baseball, and he was a driver's education instruction. On the weekends he worked for the National Guard as a firearms instructor. And on Sundays he taught Sunday school with Barbara at the Baptist Church that they both were devoted members to.

Barbara Stager's life revolved around the church. She was involved, heavily, in a great deal of church activities. Whether it was youth activities, senior's events, or other charitable affairs, Barbara was often the first to volunteer to assist.

They appeared to be the perfect image of a happy couple. No one could say that they didn't appear to be happy together.

In the early years of their marriage they both spent extravagantly, catching the attention of their friends and co-workers. They had a beach house and a large family home. They were frequently purchasing new clothes and new cars. One friend joked, "When their car needed an oil change they just got a new car". That was the frequency that they purchased vehicles. They also became members of a very prestigious, local country club to add to their symbol of wealth.

Russ's co-workers were baffled by how he could afford this lifestyle on a teacher's salary and speculation began to spread about the type of payout Barbara must have received from the death of her first husband. The belief was that it must have been fairly substantial in order for them to spend and live the way they did.

They were a perfect couple. They were dedicated to each other. They were happy in their public life together. They were devout and dedicated Christians. They were the product of envy for many. It was all a little too good to be true.

Barbara got pregnant quickly into the marriage much to Russ's pleasure and surprise, but unfortunately she miscarried the child. This weighed heavily on Russ, who wanted children very badly. However, he later adopted Barbara's two sons as his own and spent his spare time raising them as he would his own sons. Russ felt that they needed a father figure in their life and that since they had lost their father at such a young age it was his job to fill that void. They were a complete family in image and legality at that point.

Barbara soon began a job at the local radio station as an advertisement sales person and she also revealed to Russ and their friends that she was working on a novel. This novel, titled 'Untimely Death', was about the death of her husband. She claimed that she had heard back from a major publishing company that wanted to pick up her novel and had offered her a sizable cash advance.

This was the cause for major celebration in the Stager household and among their friends and family. Barbara received nothing but support in her new venture from Russ and her friends at the country club were eager to see the release of this book.

This was also the beginning of what would be an avalanche of marital problems for Russ and Barbara. Things would began to crumble soon after these happy announcements and the once perfect, happy couple will face strain and hardship like they had never believed they would in the years to come.

Suspicion and Lies

It was in the year of 1982, only a couple years into Russ and Barbara's marriage, when the truth of their situation began to become very clear. And their situation was not nearly as comfortable as Russ had been lead to believe.

Russ, while at home one afternoon, discovered a box of unpaid bills that was hidden in the house. The amount of unpaid items was staggering. The amount of debt that they were in, the amount that he was unaware of, was shocking. When he confronted Barbara about it she insisted that she would take care of it, that she was handling it, but he was reluctant to believe her.

Immediately Russ took control over the household finances, as he no longer trusted Barbara to handle it as she had before. It was clear that she hadn't been handling it at all and they desperately needed to dig themselves out of this debt. They sold their beach house. They downsized their main house, twice, in order to dig themselves out of debt, and eventually Russ had to go to his parents for financial aid.

In the mean time, Barbara approached the bank with her cash advance letter from the publishing house and on that basis alone was allowed to received a $30 000 bank loan, a loan that she has no intention of paying back.

Despite the huge level of deceit associated with the unpaid bills and the debt, Russ stayed with Barbara. He forgave her for this incident and they tried to make their marriage work again for the sake of the two boys, for the sake of their family, a family that has so recently become whole.

However, as time passed people begin to get suspicious because Barbara's book was still not released. When she was questioned about it she would be evasive and she would push off the question. Her boss at the radio station called the publishing company to inquire about the upcoming book only to find out that they had no contract with Barbara Stager or for the title in question. He immediately went to Russ and informed him of this as well as the fact that Barbara hadn't been to work at the radio station in months.

Barbara's lies were beginning to pile up and it wasn't looking good for her. However, Russ did not approach her about them. He still wanted to preserve their marriage, their family. Family mattered to him above everything else.

In 1984 the next blow to their marriage was struck when Russ discovered that Barbara was having an affair. Russ saw her, in her car, in the middle of a passionate make-out session with another man. This affair tore a major hole in their marriage despite Russ's attempts to forgive her for it.

Barbara blamed Russ for the affair. She claimed that he didn't pay enough attention to her, and that he was never around. She was also aware that he'd had an affair on his first wife and she was potentially using the guilt of that as leverage to get herself out of her own actions. It is difficult to say for certain her motivations behind this particular deceit.

Regardless of the motivation or the fault, Russ forgave her as much as he could, like he had with all things in their marriage thus far and they continued to have a life together.

But Russ was not without his suspicion in the years to come. These are suspicions he confided in his ex-wife Jo Lynn Snow whom he would meet with regularly to discuss his life and problems. He quite often talked about how he felt betrayed by the affair. He also knew that Barbara was removing large sums of money from his accounts. And he felt paranoid about his safety with Barbara the more he learned about her first marriage and the questionable circumstances of her first husband's death.

His suspicions would prove to be more than simple paranoia and his confessions to Jo Lynn would be fundamental in assuring that an alternative narrative was considered in the investigation.

Things aren't always the way they seem at first and you can't always trust the words of a grieving widow.

A Fatal Morning

It was 6:08am on February 1, 1988 when the first responders were called the Stager household. Police and EMS arrived, filled with dread at being called to the home of a friend and esteemed member of the community.

When the EMS found Russ Stager in the bedroom with a gunshot wound to the back of his head he was still breathing, barely, and had a pulse. He was rushed to the hospital to seek further medical attention where he soon died of his injuries at the age of 44.

Upon their arrival at the home Barbara Stager was distraught. She kept saying to anyone who would listen that she had warned him about "those damn guns". And she was repeating this fact over and over again. The police had to remove her from the bedroom for the EMS workers to be able to work properly.

When questioned by the police, Barbara said that she'd been trying to remove the 25-caliber pistol that Russ kept under his pillow and it had discharged. She claimed it had a hair-trigger and it had gone off before she even realized it. Barbara said that he had begun to keep the 25-caliber pistol under his pillow recently for fear of prowlers and burglars that had recently been prominent in the neighbourhood.

Barbara insisted that she hated firearms, feared them even, and that she never wanted them anywhere near the bed. She had warned him about the gun and about having guns. She was always worried that he might mistake one of the kids as a burglar and shoot them.

The incident was ruled an accidental shooting almost immediately. There was no reason to suspect foul play.

When Captain Ricky Buchanan interviewed Barbara Stager the day after the shooting he encountered Barbara's father who had already taking the sheets from the bed to be laundered. Since the shooting had been ruled accidental, there was no restriction on cleaning up the scene. Captain Buchanan found the rest of the house tidy and the bedroom to look as though nothing had even occurred there. It was unsettling, but he could not put his finger on just why it didn't sit right with him.

His impression of Barbara was not what he would have expected for a grieving widow. She was a little distraught, but she was calmer than he believed someone who had just lost her husband tragically should be. Still, she stuck to her original story about the events of the previous evening. And when Captain Buchanan left the Stager house he couldn't help but feel there was something a little off about the entire situation. He couldn't put his finger on it, but there was something that was not quite right.

It was Jo Lynn Snow that would lead the police in the correct direction for this case. When she received word that Russ Stager had died in an 'accidental' shooting she knew that there was no truth in that. Russ had been obsessive about gun safety and she knew that he would never store a firearm loaded, let alone store it with the safety off, cocked, and with a round in the chamber. And there was no way he would keep a firearm underneath a pillow. It just wouldn't have happened.

Coupled with everything that Russ had confided in her in the last few years, Jo Lynn set out to compose a letter to the police department outlining everything she knew about Russ and Barbara's marriage and Russ's suspicions.

The word of a paranoid ex-wife was not enough to sway the investigating officer, until Jo Lynn pointed out that Barbara's first husband, ten years earlier, had also died of an accidental shooting. It was at this point that interests were peaked and suspicions were raised.

Some things in life were coincidence, but when it comes to murder there are very few coincidences.

The Unraveling Story

The investigation into Russ Stager's death continued, the initial belief of it being an accidental shooting suspended until further investigation can be done. Barbara maintained her original story. She reached under the pillow, withdrew the firearm, and it accidentally discharged.

Accidental shootings are common when firearms are improperly stored or kept in unsafe places. Barbara's story is plausible. However, when it is looked at under a microscope every aspect of it begins to fall apart.

Firearms expert Eugene Bishop investigated Barbara's claim that the gun had a hair-trigger. He examined the 25-caliber Beretta pistol and subjected it to a trigger test where weight is added to the trigger in one-pound increments until the weapon fires. It was determined that the firearm had a four-pound draw weight. This indicated that it would have required deliberate force to fire the pistol and that it would not have discharged if Barbara had just 'accidentally' touched the trigger as she claimed. This was the first hole in her story.

Additionally, Eugene Bishop test fired the weapon to determine where the spent casing would land. It was determined that the casing would land to the right and rear of the shooter. Looking at the photos from the crime scene, this did not match the position of the casing, which should have been near the middle of the bedspread to match Barbara's account, but was, instead, near the pillows. This indicated that the gun was either fired from a different position than Barbara claimed or that the bullet casing was moved after the weapon was fired. This was the second hole her story.

This discrepancy was further supported by a report from medical investigators that came out following the autopsy on Russ Stager's body. The bullet wound in the back of Russ's head did not match the situation that Barbara had described. The bullet's trajectory was wrong. The angle of the trajectory indicated that the shooter would have had to been above and behind Russ when firing the weapon, therefore firing it at a downward angle. For the trajectory to match Barbara's story of firing it from the bed, the trajectory would have been up from bed level and to the back of his head. This was not so. This was the third hole in her story.

To further confirm the trajectory of the bullet they re-examined the bed sheets that were on the bed when Russ Stager was shot. If the weapon had been fired from where Barbara indicated it had been then there would be gun shot residue on the bed sheets. This could be detected despite the fact that the sheets had been laundered. Despite being tested thoroughly, the investigators could find no gun shot residue on the sheets to indicate that the firearm had been discharged from the position that Barbara had indicated. This supported the theory that the weapon had indeed been fired from above and away from the bed. This further eroded the story that she had told.

In order to test out this ongoing theory Captain Buchanan had Barbara reenact the events of that evening in front of a video camera. Captain Buchanan went as far as to say, "I'm standing face to face with a killer. I know it, but she don't know I know it." He additionally added after the filming was complete, "there's no doubt at all that she intentionally shot and killed Russ Stager, no doubt."

When reviewing the videotape it became clear almost instantly that there were inconsistencies in her narrative. She kept trying to reposition the body and readjust herself to make the facts fit. And the story she was telling began to change and become less certain for the first time since it had all started.

The chips were pilling up against Barbara Stager, but there was still some digging left to be done. They needed to find a motivation. There needed to be more evidence. So they followed the money.

Barbara had a history of hiding debt and money from Russ, but the extent that was uncovered was shocking. Barbara had taken out a second loan to cover the coast of her first loan and she had brought the documentation home in order to obtain her husband's signature. Russ's will had recently been revised and there was a life insurance policy that had been taken out on Russ, also recently. In addition, several checks had been made out from Russ's account to Barbara's account for large sums of money. The suspicion around this was growing.

The police had Durward Matheny, a forensic documents examiner, review the second bank loan, the will, and the checks that had been put through just months before Russ Stager's death. He concluded that the second bank loan held a forged signature, the revised will held a forged signature, and the checks had also been forged. In addition, the life insurance policy, for which Barbara was the sole beneficiary for $200 000, all of his assets, and their $120 000 home, was also a forged document.

The evidence was staggering, but there was one last item to be discovered. In a locker at the high school Russ Stager worked at was a cassette tape that held his final words, recorded January 29, 1988 at 1:50pm. On the cassette Russ voiced his concerns about Barbara. He talked about how she would wake him up to give him what she indicated was Aspirin and then would stand there until he took it. He would never take it. "Why, if I was asleep at 4:30 in the morning, would Barbara wake me up to give me sleeping pills?" he pondered to the audio recording. He talked about the death of her first husband and how he had begun to wonder about its legitimacy. He began to wonder if it had been accidental. And he spoke about her affair.

In the end, Barbara Stager was arrested April 15, 1988 for murder in the first degree of her husband Russell Stager.

Trail and Sentencing

The trial for Barbara Stager concluded on August 30, 1989 with a charge of first-degree murder and a sentence of death.

Barbara's attorney's stressed that she was a devout, churchgoing woman throughout the trial and tried to play on the jury's sympathies. They also indicated that she cooperated fully with law enforcement throughout the whole process and willingly complied with all requests that were made of her. They additionally argued that Barbara was a good mother, a good friend, and an upstanding member of the community. They continued to indicate that she had no criminal record up to this point and there were no mitigating factors to encourage this behaviour. In short, the defence did its job to the best of its ability.

Surprisingly, it was Jason Stager, 14 at the time when he testified about the events of that day, presented a key piece of information in debunking the timeline of his mother's narrative and solidifying her sentence.

He told the court "I was taking a shower when I heard a popping noise. I thought it was the toilet lid dropping. I finished my showed and was getting out when my mother came in and told me that Dad had been hurt. She said I needed to call 911". Jason went on to say he'd been woken up by his alarm clock and then preceded to have a shower.

The timeline presented here varied greatly from what Barbara was saying. Barbara indicated that she had fired the gun at the same time as her son's alarm going off. This testimony came out when the defence called on friends and family to testify to Barbara's good character. Unfortunately, that seemed to backfire on them.

The evidence against Barbara Stager was staggering. The jury deliberated for a grand total of forty-four minutes before they decided on this sentence: guilty.

The sentence of death was changed when it was appealed to a higher court, as all death sentences are, and it was reduced to life in prison. This was due to a technicality in the first hearing. Barbara Stager would be eligible for parole in twenty years as required by the current laws at the time of her sentencing.

Time is Not Enough

In 2009, the first parole date for Barbara Stager rolled around and twenty years was not enough for the town of Durham, North Carolina to forget what had happened to one of its most beloved members. Family members, lawyers, and police officers travelled to the North Carolina Correctional Institute for Women where Barbara Stager had resided for the last twenty years to appeal to the parole board against her release.

"I believe Barbara is a serial killer," Jo Lynn Snow maintains and she maintains that prison is the best place for her.

"She got away with the first one. She thought she could do it a second time, and she didn't make it," said Captain Buchanan. He stands by the fact that Barbara Stager has an evil nature to her. "The former Sunday school teacher has a way of gaining trust that makes her especially dangerous. She's a pillar of the community during the day, but behind closed doors at nigh, she's another woman. She's evil."

Her parole was denied in 2009. Whether this was because of the countless efforts of the family members of Russ Stager, the police involved in the investigation, and the lawyers involved in the case it is difficult to say. Regardless, the parole board did not see it fit to release her back into the public.

Her parole was denied again in 2012 with the parole board making the same decision and her parole hearing was postponed in 2015.

Barbara Stager was up for a new parole hearing on August 1, 2017 and the results of this hearing have yet to hit the media.

KILLER COUNTESS : THE TRUE STORY OF JAMILA M'BAREK

122

HAILEY FOSTER

She was rumored to be the prostitute lover of such celebrities as George Clooney and Bruce Willis. But in 2004, Jamila M'Barek would make headlines of her own.

Her name would be thrust into the spotlight when her sixty-four-year-old lover, Anthony Ashley-Cooper, the 10th Earl of Shaftsbury went missing. Five months later, he would found dead within a deep ravine at the foot of the French Alps, his horribly decomposed body half-eaten by wild animals.

Fingers of blame soon pointed to two unlikely suspects.

The exotic and beautiful Tunisian escort, Jamila M'Barek and her stoic brother, Muhammad M'Barek. The question was, what singular thread linked a rich, playboy aristocrat, a psychopathic petty criminal and a prostitute from the French Riviera?

The answer – one had a lust for money, the other had a lust for sex...

EARLY LIFE

Jamila M'Barek was born in 1961 in the storied and tiny northern commune of Lens, Pas de Calais in France. Despite the beautiful and seemingly idyllic surroundings, young Jamila's life was anything but peaceful due to the temper tantrums of her father, a violent binge drinking alcoholic. To escape her miserable homelife, Jamila and her six siblings (the eighth died at seven months of age) ran away from the home with her mother. The matriarch of the family brought them to the Arabic speaking Republic of Tunisia in Northern Africa after securing a divorce.

Free from her abusive father, the family felt security for the first time. But this was but a momentary illusion, for they could only afford to live in the most unsavory of slums and were readily ostracized due to the fact that divorce is considered wholly taboo by popular Tunisian society.

"Our neighbors rejected us because they saw us as foreigners," Jamila's sister Fatima said. "Because they knew how bad of a man our father was, and most of all because my parents were divorced."

"This ostracization made an indelible imprint on Jamila's mind," forensic psychologist Paula Orange said. "She hated the fact that her family was looked down upon. She would be willing to do whatever it took to not only gain power but influence. In the years ahead, this would mean using her body."

Jamila was determined to get ahead. She had a great deal of intellectual savvy and graduated near the top of her class.

"Jamila is very intelligent, always was," Fatima said. "She was always in the top two in her class and at the end of the school year, she received a prize, [every year] without fail. She was our role model. We always wanted to be like Jamila."

The adoration Jamila received from her family, however, would not last for very long. When she was only seventeen, Jamila moved to the former military stronghold town of Sant-Troupès, where she fell into a torrid relationship with a rich businessman from the Netherlands named Raf Schouten. Jamila became pregnant and bore Schouten both a son, named Raf in honor of the father, and a daughter, Kiara, and for a time the marriage was a happy one.

But Jamila wanted more money than even the rich Raf was giving her. Inexplicably, the rich man's wife turned to prostitution.

"It is a head scratcher," Orange said. "Until you take into account the trauma Jamila experienced in her upbringing. Money in and of itself would not be able to fill that psychological wound she experienced from being treated like a third-class citizen. Neither did having children. What she wanted was validation in the eyes of the world. A status that she could acquire. Prostitution gave her a sort of status as she would be wooed by high-status clientele."

Raf soon learned of Jamila's sordid nightly escapades, feeling shock and repulsion. He tried to talk her out of it but she only increased her activity.

"Jamila was equally as sick as all of her lovers," Orange said. "She could enjoy sex only when she was getting paid for it. That in and of itself was a peculiar fetish for her."

Raf could not handle the infidelity. He filed for a divorce.

Free from marital restraints and motherhood duties, Jamila plunged ahead with her hedonistic lifestyle. Word spread of the sexy North African with the great breasts and legs...not to mention her skills in the bedroom. Rumors of her sexual prowess would reach Hollywood circles. Word of her beauty eventually reached the heads of Playboy Magazine who solicited her for a nude photo shoot.

Jamila posed for the magazine in 1993 and the exposure allowed her to climb the social ladder while entering into an elite female escort service. She would be catering to a very specific and wealthy clientele, many of whom were rumored to have been foreign dignitaries and Hollywood playboys (including such celebrities as George Clooney and Bruce Willis).

THE BARON

Not long after joining this escort agency Jamila would meet the man who would change her life forever.

In the intermittent time between her first marriage and her second, Jamila retained a great deal of her wealth, owning two properties in affluent communities, one in Tunisia, the other in Cannes, France. She favored flashy, expensive clothing and lived the high life, making thousands of dollars per night.

"Jamila had a weird attraction to older men," Orange said. "She made it clear to her agency that she preferred them older and of course, rich."

The agency would oblige her when the Baron came into the city. He had heard of Jamila's reputation and wanted very much to meet her. After the agency hinted at how much money he had, she almost bolted out of the door to meet the mysterious older man who was awaiting her in Versailles.

En route, however, she found herself caught in a rain storm, the gusty weather mussing up her hair and clothes. Arriving at her destination, she realized who the palatial estate belonged to.

Anthony Tony Ashley-Cooper, the 10th Earl of Shaftsbury, Baron of Wimborne St. Giles and Baron of Pawlett, a descendant to one of the most recognized noble families in all of Britain.

"The Baron or The Duke, whatever you want to call him," Orange said. "Was the stereotypical bored rich guy. He moved to Paris where he didn't do anything but drink all day and have sex with high-end prostitutes."

Jamila arrived at his palace door, rain-soaked and looking like a mess. But the Baron paid her appearance no mind.

Upon her entrance, the Baron ushered Jamila into his foyer with a flurry of apologies, saying that it was all his fault that she had to weather such deplorable conditions.

The Baron was old but well-dressed, at least for what his role was on the French Riviera and that was of a well-to-do solicitor of prostitutes. He wore black leather pants, pink silk shirts and alligator skin shoes. This would all be topped off by a gold chain around his neck.

To Jamila's surprise, her first meeting with the Baron would be completely platonic.

"The Baron was content to just talk about himself," Orange said. "He talked about his family, his antiques, his paintings."

He ordered some pizza and gave Jamila some wine as they chatted away.

Jamila would fall asleep within a few hours, worn out by alcohol and the long-winded nature of the Baron's personality. But the Baron would wake her up early in the morning and their conversation continued.

After this initial date, a relationship quickly blossomed between them, one which was not entirely driven by the prospect of either sex nor payment. The Baron came across as a perfect client, he was harmless and fun. He did have one peculiar idiosyncrasy, as during the sex sessions with Jamila he would inexplicably shout out "Oh Mommy!"

Jamila, however, didn't care. The old man could call her whatever he wanted as long as she was paid and taken care of.

"They both had their own Oedipal complexes," Orange said. "The Baron obsessed on his mother. He had lost his grip on reality after she died." "You remind me of my mom," he would tell all of his lovers.

After sex, the Baron would ask his prostitute lover to read to him from a chapter in a book. His favorite? The biography of Napoleon.

"Of course, Jamila had her own Oedipal complex going on," Orange said. "She only got turned on by older men. She had to fill that hole left by her abusive father. She found a Daddy replacement in the Baron."

A LONG-TERM DEAL

Their relationship continued over the next few months until Jamila informed the Baron that she was pregnant.

"I don't want him to be a bastard," she said, reminding him of her own troubles as the product of a divorce.

"She put the Baron on the spot," Orange said. "He had no intentions of every marrying and his entire life was one of debauchery. His family got word of what happened and vehemently warned him against marrying the gold-digging prostitute from North Africa."

He didn't listen and the two would marry in a small but extravagant ceremony in the Netherlands.

The Baron would dote on his bride, showering her with gifts such as a custom-made windmill placed upon a lavish villa. He hired a staff of attendees and gave her a spending allotment of $100,000 per month.

"Orange made the mistake that most rich men make," Orange said. "Number one, he had no idea he was being played and wrote Jamila into his will."

Upon his death, Jamila would gain four million Euros as well as two pieces of high-end real estate in Nice.

VALIDATION

With the marriage to royalty, Jamila finally acquired the status she always craved. Or so she thought.

She began touting her title of "Countess" and was absolutely overjoyed to discover that she had her own street. Becoming instantly infatuated with her newfound status as literal royalty, Jamila shortly demanded her husband to take her to his ancestral home in St. Giles House in Dorset, a request which the kindly Earl readily obliged. However, the welcome she would receive would not be a warm one. When the Jamila opened the door, the couple was greeted by an elderly English housekeeper, or rather, the Baron was greeted, while Jamila was coldly ignored. This trend would continue through the exploration of the creaky manor until it reached such a point that the new Countess became quite flustered. However, she reached her breaking point when she was informed by one of Shaftsbury's son's that the house was reserved for the family heir, not the family heiress. Utterly indignant at her poor treatment and a figurative slap in the face, Jamila left in a rental car.

"It was a groundhog day moment for Jamila," Orange said. "She was disrespected yet again and it brought back memories of her days in Tunisia where she was invisible to everyone around her. She thought she had acquired the status she had longed for her whole life. Instead, she was treated like a nothing."

Jamila would never visit the old manor again.

A BUYER'S REMORSE

The Earl began having anxiety about his upcoming fatherhood. Would the child cramp his style? Would Jamila lose her tight body with the pregnancy? Thoughts like that raged through his head until one day he realized that Jamila looked the same. In fact, as she lounged around the pool area she looked as fit and firm as ever.

The Earl began to worry, it had been seven months since the wedding! Where was the baby bump?

Jamila assured her confused husband that she was simply the kind of woman upon whom pregnancy just did not show. The Earl was far from convinced and now the relationship began to take a turn for the worse.

"They began fighting," Orange said. "Ironically, their relationship had been a congenial one until the day the Baron had brought her to the manor. But now they began to fight. He had that feeling that her pregnancy was part of a ruse. A ruse to get money out of him."

Jamila would tell him that she had gotten an abortion. She further insulted him by saying that she would never have a child with a man who was a drug addict, alcoholic, sex pervert who called his lovers "mother" before his orgasms.

The Baron became furious, now realizing that his suspicions were spot on.

"He tried to kick her out of the house," Orange said. "She fought back. That is the amazing part. She thought she was entitled to whatever he had given her. That somehow it was her right to be called a 'Countess.'"

The Baron had given her something she didn't have before.

Status.

She had money with Raf but was still nothing more than his wife. But with the Baron, she was not merely the wife of a rich man, she was the wife of a noble – a descendant of British royalty. So alluring and seductive was this idea to Jamila that she would regularly wear a tiara out into public and curtly demand that all passersby refer to her as Countess or, Lady Shaftesbury. Naturally, this was not something Jamila wanted to lose.

"She begged, pleaded and threatened," Orange said. "But the Baron had made up his mind. He felt betrayed and no longer trusted the prostitute he pulled off the clubs of Versailles. She had to go."

PUBLIC HUMILIATION

Jamila then began attacking the Baron publicly, telling the newspapers of her husband's sexual perversions. She then returned to her previous life of a prostitute.

Jamila hosted lavish orgies at the Cannes flat which the Earl had gifted to her on their wedding day, one would be hard-pressed to find a more stark and venomous repudiation of a former lover. However, Jamila did maintain a small modicum of modesty, for when she began placing ads in the local newspapers for her prostitution agency she purposefully omitted the fact that she was a true Countess, deeming such a declaration to be indiscreet.

For well over a year the Earl of Shaftesbury ignored these libidinous affronts to his image, seemingly unconcerned. It appeared as if he had put Jamila completely out of his mind, that was until he met yet another stunning beauty named Nadia. Much in keeping with his passionate nature, the Earl had fallen completely head over heels for this new paramour and sought her hand in marriage.

But Jamila would not take kindly to her replacement.

Shortly after meeting Nadia, the Earl telephoned his former lover and informed her that he wanted a divorce.

Jamila responded only by saying, "You will be sorry."

Six months passed before the Earl took action, all the while Jamila continued to engage in prostitution, consorting with lecherous high-rollers and shadowy foreign dignitaries. On the fourth of November in 2004, the Earl drove took a long drive to the outskirts of Italy to garner the advice of fortune teller, a move that was much in keeping with his idiosyncratic character. He then spent a sleepless night carousing about the town before departing for the Noga Hilton of Cannes.

The next morning, Jamila received a phone call from the Earl. It was the day of their wedding anniversary and tensions were high. The Earl asked his former paramour to meet him for an early lunch to discuss the terms of their divorce. Jamila readily agreed but never showed up, leaving the Earl quite irate. He called again, perplexed and was told to meet Jamila at her apartment where they could discuss the issue in private. Thus, unshaven and groggy headed, the old adventurous aristocrat made the small pilgrimage to his former wife's apartment that sat along the storied Avenue Marechal Koenig. After making his way over the hill before the abode and through the huge, double gated entrance way, Tony Ashley-Copper, the 10th Earl of Shaftesbury was never to be seen alive again.

MURDER OF ROYALTY

The Earl entered the apartment and was given the cold shoulder by Jamila. Inside, he saw Jamila's brother, Muhammad M'barek. Muhammad was a former professional rugby player turned petty criminal. He was small but rugged and was described by all who knew him as a "money hungry psychopath."

Little did the Baron know that Jamila had hired her brother to kill him.

Her reasoning was that the Baron would file for divorce and her assets and inheritance, as well as her lauded title, would be irrevocably stripped from her in one single, fell swoop.

An argument quickly erupted and ended with Muhammad attacking the Earl. The older man was slammed to the floor and was no much for the vicious younger man. Muhammad squeezed the Baron's throat so forcibly that he snapped the Earl's neck, killing him instantly.

The brother and sister murder team threw the old man's body into their car. They drove to the base of the French Alps and tossed his body into a deep ravine.

For six months, not a single soul heard any word of the whereabouts of the Earl. However, the silence was broken during the ensuing police investigation with Jamila initially claiming that if anyone had killed her husband it was the youthful beauty, Nadia, the Earl's newest and last love. However, this theory didn't hold water, for

Nadia stood to gain nothing from the Earl's demise, as she was not written into his will.

What was clear was that Jamila stood to gain millions.

The police came next for her brother, Muhammad, at his residence at Munich. Muhammad, unsurprisingly, corroborated his sister's tale, saying that a fight did indeed break out between himself and the Earl, but that the old man's death had been but a tragic accident, a cruel twist of the fates. As the evidence mounted, the murderous duo's confidence began to crumble, slowly eroding away, bit by bit, piece by piece like the sonorous waves of the ocean slow-rending some ancient shale cliff-face.

Eventually, Jamila broke down in a hysterical fit and declared that she could no longer hide the truth, that her brother had indeed killed the Earl in a fight, but with the peculiar caveat that it had all just been a terrible accident. This did not fly either, for phone records show very clearly that it was nothing short of cold-blooded murder. The judge considered the case for but two scant hours before coming to a verdict.

Guilty on all counts.

After the terse hearing, both Jamila and her brother Muhammad were sentenced to twenty-five years of imprisonment, and for many years no word was heard from either of them.

Jamila, in particular, utterly refused any and all solicitations for interviews from the media and independent journalists and researchers alike. All the while maintaining her innocence and never expressing even the slightest shred of regret or remorse – in her mind, it was all just one terrible accident, a poor joke, an unforeseen twist of fate.

To this day she remains imprisoned and demands that the inmates and prison guards refer to her by the title she legally retains, "Countess Jamila M'Barek."

JUDY BUENOANO

Judy Buenoano loved men. But she loved killing them more.

In 1971, she murdered her husband James and nine years later she would kill her own son, Michael. In 1983, she would attempt but fail to kill her boyfriend, John Gentry. She is also believed to have been responsible for the death of Bobby Joe Morris (another boyfriend) in 1978. She was never convicted of the Morris crime, however, as by the time the authorities had connected the dots she was sentenced to death for the murder of her first husband.

But the suspicions didn't stop with the Morris death. Buenoano is also suspected of killing a man in 1974 and in 1980, another boyfriend would die under suspicious circumstances.

Buenoano would become the first woman executed in Florida since 1848 and only the third woman executed since capital punishment had been reinstated in 1976.

She would be sent to the electric chair in 1998. Her last words were that she wanted to be remembered as a "good mother."

Instead, she would go down as one of the most sadistic female serial killers in American history.

This is her story.

EARLY LIFE

Judy was born Judias Welty in Quanah, Texas on April 4th, 1943. Her father was a day laborer at a local farm. Judy would talk about her mother being a full-blooded member of the Mesquite Apache tribe but little did she know that a "Mesquite Apache" tribe didn't exist.

Her mother would die of tuberculosis when Judy was only two years old. She and her baby brother Robert would be sent to live with their grandparents while their two older siblings would be put up for adoption.

"When Judy's mother died," forensic psychologist Paula Orange said. "It sent Judy's life into a tailspin. This is one of those 'Butterfly

Effect' scenarios. A tragic circumstance that occurred early in a child's life that led to her perpetuating pain on everyone else for the rest of her own adult life."

She would eventually leave her grandparents and join her father in Roswell, New Mexico. He had remarried and Judy would claim that both he and her new stepmother would beat, starve, and burn her with cigarettes.

They made her a "house slave", forcing her to do chores around the house at their bidding. Judy would finally act out at the age of fourteen as she would burn two of her step brothers with hot grease. Not stopping there, she attacked both her father and step-mom with fists flying.

Police would be called and Judy would be jailed for over two months. After she served her jail time, the judge gave Judy a choice, either return home or go to reform school. She opted for the latter and was sent to Foothills High School. She would remain there until 1959 when she would graduate at the age of sixteen.

She held her entire family in contempt, particularly her younger brother Robert.

"I wouldn't spit down his throat if his guts were on fire," Judy once said when asked about her brother.

CHANGING IDENTITY

Judy returned to Roswell but changed her name to "Anna Schultz". She found work as a nurse aide and would give birth to a baby boy out of wedlock, Michael Schultz on March 30, 1961. Judy would remain silent on the identity of the baby's father but people believed that Judy was having an affair with a pilot from the nearby air force base.

In 1963, the twenty-two-year-old Judy would marry James Goodyear. Goodyear was twenty-nine years old and serving as a sergeant in the United States Air Force.

They would have their first child together, James Jr, four years later. James would celebrate the event by legally adopting Michael. Daughter

Kimberly would come a year later as the family would move to Orlando, Florida.

Judy would then open her own business, starting the Conway Acres Child Care Center in Orlando. She listed James as the co-owner even though he was during a one-year tour in the Vietnam War. After returning home, he only had three months of downtime before he was admitted to the U.S. Naval Hospital in Orlando, complaining from symptoms staff physicians never quite identified. He would die on September 15, 1971.

Goodyear was only thirty-seven years old at the time of death and authorities believed he died due to natural causes.

"He came home from Vietnam ill and he never got well," Judy said. ``It had nothing to do with me. I was not in Vietnam."

"Crazy that Goodyear was able to survive the horrors of Vietnam but not Judy Buenoano," Orange said. "He had no idea he was married to a sociopath. She had no respect for the fact that he had just put himself on the line for her and the country. All she saw were dollar signs."

Judy poisoned James with arsenic and waited almost a week after his death before cashing in his three life insurance policies. A few months later, an "accidental fire" burned down their Orlando home. Judy would receive another $90,000 in fire insurance.

She lost her husband and her home. But her purse was never fatter.

NO GRIEVING WIDOWS ALLOWED

Judy would waste no time finding another man. Despite having three kids in tow, she would find a new love in Bobby Joe Morris when she moved her family to Pensacola.

It was business as usual for Judy as she had a fat bank account courtesy of James Goodyear and a new beau in Bobby Joe. Eldest son Michael, however, was not doing well in school. He scored on the low end on IQ tests and was a behavioral problem. Judy would get him evaluated at a state hospital in 1974 and then sent Michael out to foster care where he would also receive psychiatric treatment.

Judy's new home would suffer another "accidental fire" and she collected money from the insurance. She then took Michael out of foster care and moved to Trinidad, Colorado with Bobby Joe and the rest of her children. Judy then changed her name from "Anna Schultz" to "Judias Morris".

FOUR YEARS MAX

Judy would date Bobby Joe for four years before deciding it was time to cut him loose.

Bobby Joe would start to suffer from the same mysterious illness as James Goodyear did years earlier as he complained of dizziness and vomiting. He would be admitted to San Rafael Hospital on January 4, 1978, but doctors would not be able to pinpoint what was wrong with him. He would be sent home to Judy's care two weeks later. Two days later, however, he would would pitch face-first into his dinner plate, unconscious. He would be rushed to the hospital, but Judy knew that her "medicine" had taken effect.

Five days later, Bobby Joe Morris would be dead. Doctors would chalk up his death to cardiac arrest and metabolic acidosis.

Judy would wait, just like she did after she killed James, before cashing in on Bobby Joe's life insurance.

Authorities were none the wiser.

But Bobby Joe's family suspected something fishy was going on. Back in 1974, Judy and Bobby Joe had been visiting Brewton, Alabama when a man from Florida was found dead in a motel room in that town. Police would find the man in the room after receiving an anonymous call. He was shot in the chest with a .22-caliber weapon and his throat was cut open.

Judy's connection to the crime? Bobby Joe's mother had overheard Judy telling her son about the murder.

"The sonofabitch shouldn't have come up here in the first place," Judy said. "If he came up here he was gonna die."

Bobby Joe had told his mother about the crime on his deathbed. She thought the confession could be attributed to his delirium, but Bobby Joe told her too many specifics to ignore.

"We should never had done that terrible thing," Bobby Joe mumbled to his mother. "Never should have done that to him."

She tipped off police but they would not be able to find any fingerprints inside the room and no bullet was recovered from the corpse. The case remained unsolved.

WHAT'S ONE MORE SURNAME?

On May 3rd, 1978, Judy would change her name again. This go around, she would change her last name to Buenoano, which in Spanish meant "good year." She stated that she meant it as a tribute to her husband James Goodyear and her Apache mother.

Things continued to go bad with Michael as he dropped out of high school in the tenth grade. With limited employment opportunities, he would join the army in June of 1979 and get assigned to Ft. Benning in Georgia after basic training. When he was on his way to his new post, he visited Judy in Pensacola.

Judy greeted her son with open arms. Then she began poisoning him.

By the time he reached Ft. Benning, he felt sick. Army physicians would find seven times the normal level of arsenic in his body.

They could do little to reverse the damage done. Six weeks after his arrival, the muscles in his arms and legs and deteriorated to the point where he was a paraplegic.

"Michael had no use of his legs," Orange said. "And he could not move his arms past his elbow. Again, Judy was a sociopath. It is unfathomable for a normal human being, a mother, to do this to her own child. Yet she did it to Michael. He was always an inconvenience to her but now that he had military insurance he could become an asset in death."

Judy would give Michael the short shrift while favoring James and Kimberly. Michael and James didn't get along well as clearly their mother favored the latter. Judy would hide Michael when people came over because she was ashamed of him. She would have a neighbor named Constance Lang watch over him when visitors arrived.

"Michael didn't fit the picture Judy wanted to present to the world," Orange said. "She wanted to be looked at like a woman of high status. She drove a Corvette and owned her own business. Michael was a slow-thinking kid. She didn't want anyone to see that."

The army didn't investigate the reasons behind Michael's inordinate levels of arsenic. Instead, they set him up with leg braces and a prosthetic device on one of his arms.

He would be discharged from active duty because of the medical disability.

But his mother saw dollar signs.

The day after his return home, Judy wasted no time. She organized a fishing trip with Michael, James, and daughter Kimberly. They would leave Kimberly ashore at the East River bridge while they went into the water with a two-seat canoe. A small folding lawn chair had been placed in the middle of the canoe for Michael who had was outfitted with a leg brace, a fishing reel, and a ski belt.

James would state that had fished for about two hours when they were reaching shore when a "snake fell into the canoe." He said that everyone panicked as the snake slithered around. The canoe hit a log and capsized.

James would claim to have been knocked out by the impact and would remember nothing until he came to inside an ambulance.

He would tell this version to the court but when he was talking to Army investigators, he made no mention of a snake.

"There is conjecture as to how much James was involved or much did he know," Orange said. "The statement given to the army investigators is different from what he would state later in court. The statement given to the army was a written statement and the handwriting didn't seem to match his own."

A man named Ricky Hicks saw the overturned canoe, an ice chest, and a plastic bag in the river. He also saw Judy and James.

"I lost the other boy," Judy said as Ricky approached them on the shore. "A snake had gotten into the canoe and I tried to hold the snake down with a paddle."

"Where is he?"

"It's no use," Judy said, waving him off.

Hicks said Judy appeared to be concerned about James then asked him for a beer. He then drove Judy's car to a nearby phone and called the county rescue squad.

The rescue team arrived and began looking for the missing Michael.

The canoe had not moved as there was barely a current. They would find Michael's body one-quarter of a mile upriver where the canoe had been rescued. The rescuers stated that it should not have been a problem to swim upstream, suggesting that Michael could have been saved.

Judy initially said that Michael had a life jacket on but later recanted and said that it was a ski belt.

There was no ski belt on Michael when he was found.

Judy would later state that after the canoe capsized, she saw James lying face down in the water. She swam over and cleared his air passage to resuscitate him. She looked around for Michael then was picked up by Ricky Hicks.

"Michael disappeared under water," Judy said. "I went to rescue James. I almost lost both of my sons that day. Mothers just don't murder their children. If I'd have lost both of them, I don't know what I would have done. They would have had to put me in a mental institution."

"Kimberly's boyfriend would later testify that Judy had killed Michael for the insurance money," Orange said. "The children knew about their mother but she had clearly brainwashed them into silence. She provided for them, she fed them. She knew what was best."

Telling the police that she was a "clinical physician", they bought her story of the boat capsizing. The army investigators did not buy her account. Not having any evidence, however, they would eventually pay her Michael's military life insurance ($20,000). Investigators got suspicious, however, when they found out that two civilian life policies were taken out on Michael. The applications on both policies look to have been forged.

Judy's former sister-in-law, Peggy Goeller, would call to inquire how she was doing. She would make no mention of Michael's death during her first call but on a second call she told Peggy that Michael had died "during Army maneuvers".

MOVING ON

Judy would demonstrate very little grief over Michael's death and she would not be charged with his murder. Foremost on her mind was finding another man and another big check.

She opened a beauty salon in Gulf Breeze and found her next mark: businessman John Gentry.

Gentry was more well-heeled than her previous conquests so Judy put on airs for his sake. She told him that she had Ph.D.'s in biochemistry and psychology and was the former head of nursing at West Florida Hospital.

Gentry believed her story and decided to spoil his blue-blooded girlfriend expensive gifts, vacations and the finest cuisine all in the name of courtship.

Pushing the envelope, Judy would encourage John to provide life insurance for both them both. She then secretly boosted Gentry's coverage from $50,000 to $500,000 without him knowing.

Two months later, Judy began giving Gentry "vitamin pills".

"Come on," she said, placing two pills into Gentry's palm.

"What are you, my mother?" Gentry asked.

"Well, God forbid I want to see you healthy," Judy slid the cup of water toward her prey.

Gentry would then complain of dizziness and later begin vomiting after his daily dose of Judy's "vitamins."

He would admit himself into the hospital and noticed that his symptoms disappeared when he stopped taking the vitamins.

Still smitten by Judy, he did not suspect her of wrongdoing. Instead, he took her vitamins and hid them in his briefcase.

One night, however, Judy sat him down for a special dinner. She had a very special announcement.

"I'm pregnant," she said, smiling in triumph.

"Finally," Gentry said. He told Judy that they should celebrate. She told him to go to the liquor store for an expensive bottle of champagne.

"Be right back," he said, kissing her with excitement.

Running out the door, Gentry got into his car and a bomb exploded with he turned the ignition key.

Amazingly, Gentry survived the blast as trauma surgeons saved his life.

"Judy really overplayed her hand with the explosion in the car," Orange said. "Really it speaks to her level of dedication and ingenuity. Who knows where she got the idea, maybe watching the Godfather. But the police found the dynamite residue inside Gentry's car. They decided to look no further than to Judy herself."

Their interrogation and research would unearth lie after lie. They found out about the $450,000 increase in Gentry's life insurance.

Gentry himself thought the insurance had been canceled. He was shocked to learn that she had increased the payout and was paying his premiums out of her own pocket. The police didn't spare him any quarter. They would him that she was not a real doctor and that she couldn't get pregnant.

"What?" Gentry muttered, completely flabbergasted.

Judy had been sterilized seven years earlier.

Gentry couldn't believe his ears. Police would go on to say that she had booked tickets for a world cruise for herself and her children...leaving Gentry out. They discovered that Judy had been telling her friends that Gentry was suffering from a "terminal illness."

The only "terminal illness" Gentry had was Judy Buenoano.

Now fully convinced, Gentry would reach into his briefcase and give police the "vitamin pills" that Judy had been giving him.

"Judy was emptying the vitamin casing and filling it with formaldehyde and a little arsenic," Orange said. "Over time, this would have been lethal."

The state attorney would refuse to charge Judy as they wanted an air tight case in order to prosecute. Knowing that they had their killer, officers, and federal agents searched Judy's home in Gulf Breeze, obtaining wire and tape from her bedroom that looked to match the same wire/tape they found on the bomb in Gentry's car.

They would search her son James' room, finding marijuana and a sawed-off shotgun. He would be jailed him for possession of drugs and an illegal weapon.

"Again, this is a strange mistake on Judy's part," Orange said. "She was meticulous and a good liar. Why she didn't remove any and all evidence from her home is a head-scratcher. She had gotten sloppy because she had gotten away with so many crimes before without so much as a slap on the wrist. She thought she was above the law, got careless and left incriminating evidence behind."

Judy would then be arrested at her beauty salon and charged with attempted murder. It took a month of police work, but authorities would trace the source of the dynamite used in the bomb, linking the Alabama buyer to Judy via phone records which showed numerous long-distance calls from her home.

Judy would pay bail but authorities would not let up. Five months later, she would be indicted for first-degree murder in the death of her son Michael, with an additional count of grand theft for the insurance scam.

Feeling the noose around her neck, Judy would fake a seizure and wind up in Santa Rosa Hospital.

Authorities then exhumed the bodies of the men they believed she killed. Bobby Joe Morris was exhumed with arsenic found in his remains. Identical results were obtained with the exhumation of James Goodyear, in the following month.

Connecting the dots, police obtained a court order to exhume the bodies of all the men that had died while associated with Judy; son Michael, husband James Goodyear, and boyfriend Bobby Joe Morris.

Arsenic would be found in all of the bodies.

"There was enough arsenic in him (Goodyear) to kill twelve people," Detective Ted Chamberlain said. "So he was loaded. I mean that boy was loaded with it when he went down."

OPEN AND SHUT CASE

In 1984, Judy would be convicted of the murders of Michael and attempted murder of Gentry. In a separate trial in 1985, she would be convicted of the murder of James Goodyear in which she would ultimately receive the death sentence.

Judy would be imprisoned in the Florida Department of Corrections Broward Correctional Institution death row for women.

HER FINAL HOURS

Judy would spend her last day watching a hunting and fishing show, eating chocolates, and talking about old times with her children and cousin Jeanne Eaton. She would read a suspense novel called "Remember Me" and her last meal with be steamed broccoli, asparagus, strawberries and hot tea.

Judy's impending execution did not receive the same media attention as Karla Faye Tucker whose was executed only a month earlier. Her execution was opposed by the Pope and Jesse Jackson.

'"She may not have been as photogenic, as young or as pretty as Karla, but she was just as good a Christian," Eaton said.

"Judy obviously had her enablers within her family," Orange said. "How could she be 'just as good a Christian' if she is poisoning people, blowing them up and the 'Christian' she is being compared to is ice-picking people to death. People say the strangest things."

But Judy herself was bitter that no one paid much attention to her presence on death row, particularly the fact that she was a woman.

``Karla was a young female, very attractive and she had become a Christian in prison," Judy said. ``We all prayed that she would be granted a stay of execution and clemency because we felt that she was a different person and she deserved a chance. Possibly, I am a different person. But I was a Christian when I came here. I was a devout Catholic. I've not changed in that."

"It was a bit of a curiosity as to why the media was so charged to prevent the execution of Karla Faye Tucker and paid little heed to Buenoano," Orange said. "Tucker's killings were ferocious and sadistic while Buenoano's killings could be seen as passive. But what drew people to Tucker was her physical appearance and demeanor. She came across as a sweet, reformed choir girl at the end. She had a charming smile and a soft voice. Buenoano, on the other hand, looked sinister. She had squinty eyes, high cheekbones and a snarling, Southern drawl. Her body language and demeanor screamed hostile."

Judy would enter the death chamber with several guards by her side. They strapped her into the large oak chair, placing leather straps over her waist, wrists, chest, and legs.

They fitted the calf and headpiece electrodes last, inserting a wet sponge in between to reduce the burning of Judy's skin.

"Do you have a final statement?" the warden asked.

"No, sir," Judy closed her eyes tight.

The witnesses on the other side of the glass partition watched in silence.

Judy did not look at them as a leather mask was placed over her face.

The warden nodded his head and the switch was pulled.

Steam wafted up from her right leg as her body jolted for thirty-eight seconds. Her hands balled into fists, white knuckling from the shock as smoke rose from her feet to the ceiling.

Then Judy went limp. She would be pronounced dead at 7:08 a.m., March 30th, 1998.

The date was her son Michael's 37th birthday.

The Internet Black Widow

ANITA MORRISON

Melissa Ann Shepard, also known as the internet black widow, is a cold blooded woman who has regularly been on the wrong side of the law. She was released from jail again in 2016. But, even at 82 years of age, she could still pose a very real threat to any single men that cross her path.

Melissa hasn't always been a danger to men. She was born, Melissa Ann Russell, on the 16th May 1935 in New Brunswick, Canada. Melissa's first marriage, to Russel Shepard, seemed relatively normal. The marriage lasted over two decades, before eventually ending in divorce. Perhaps this experience turned Melissa cynical, because every relationship that followed was anything but normal. Melissa and Shepard had been living in Prince Edward Island for 25 years, although she had served time in jail for fraud. In fact, there were over 30 fraud convictions between 1977 and 1991. Locally, she was thought of as a small town girl who was hungry for wealth, someone who wanted to live the high life. Still, at worst she could be described as a petty criminal. No one would ever have expected what was to follow.

In 1989, Melissa met Gordon Stewart. Stewart was 42 years old and at a vulnerable time in his life. His first wife died in 1986. It had been a successful, loving marriage. Stewart was still grieving the loss several years later, often feeling down and lonely. Having worked in the army for many years, Stewart had savings of around $50000 in the bank, plus a good pension. Gordon Stewart's sister, Kate Reeves, said that she "thought it would be wonderful if he met someone and the sooner the better. But, that feeling lasted a very short time."

When Melissa first met Stewart, she introduced herself as a devout Christian. She seemed very normal and sweet, and quickly gained Stewart's trust. Melissa was actually still married to her first husband at this time, but that didn't stop her. Although supportive at first, Stewart's friends and family started to grow suspicious when stories of her involvement in fraud began to surface. Prince Edward Island is a small place, and it's not easy to keep secrets there. Stewart's brother,

Brian, and sister, Kate Reeves, discovered that Melissa had been in and out of jail, and had used various different names. A local member of the police force even advised them that Gordon Stewart should stay away from Melissa. But, Stewart wouldn't listen. He was smitten.

The new couple married in Las Vegas and she became known as Melissa Ann Stewart. Unfortunately, the honeymoon period didn't last very long. Stewart already had a drinking habit, but it seemed to get progressively worse after he met Melissa. He also ran into some money troubles. His life savings, $50000, were disappearing fast. However, money worries quickly took a back seat when Stewart starting to experience various health problems. Stewart lost a significant amount of weight, and was regularly taken into hospital after passing out and collapsing. Doctors found drugs in his system, as well as copious amounts of alcohol. Some people assumed that he had developed a more serious addiction. However, Brian Stewart was suspicious, he found out that Melissa had access to prescription drugs and he "just knew there was something going on".

The pair seemed to bring out the worst in each other, and one night a fight broke out over money. Melissa claimed that Stewart hit her, and he served jail time for this alleged attack. Stewart's family were shocked by this and Kate Reeves claimed that "this is not an abused wife... this was an abusive, is an abusive, person herself". After spending time in jail, Stewart was released on the condition that he stayed away from Melissa. However, Melissa initiated contact again, saying that she wanted to work on their marriage.

In the early spring of 1991, the couple moved to Halifax. Stewart had agreed that a change of scenery might help their troubled marriage. Sadly, this wasn't to be. After only one week in Halifax, they set off on a weekend drive from which only one would return.

The couple drove to a secluded area. Later toxicology reports showed that Stewart had a lethal amount of alcohol and prescription drugs in his system, and experts believed that he would have been unable to function. However, Melissa claimed that another argument broke out, again about money. She alleged that, following the argument, Stewart attacked and raped her. In order to escape from him, she jumped back into the car and tried to drive away. Apparently, she accidentally reversed over her husband, thinking he was a log. She then accelerated over him again, and drove off quickly. Two people witnessed the horrific events, and watched as Melissa left the scene. Gordon Stewart was dead.

Melissa drove to a police station, and told them that she wanted to report a rape. Almost as an afterthought, she added that she had killed the perpetrator – her husband. According to police, this immediately aroused suspicion. Why wouldn't she have remained at the scene to explain her story? Suspicion grew when it was discovered that there was no evidence of rape, or any kind of attack on Melissa, and toxicology reports showed that it was unlikely Stewart was even conscious at the time. The outcome of the investigation was that Melissa's motive for killing Stewart had been monetary, not in self-defence. Stewart had a large pension and, as his wife, Melissa would have been eligible for various benefits. Despite the evidence stacked up against her, Melissa told a compelling story in court, painting a picture of a violent marriage and a battered woman. She was convicted only of manslaughter, and was given a six year sentence.

Before she had even been released from jail, Melissa started to use the situation to her advantage. She became a poster girl for women's rights and starred in a major documentary about escaping abusive marriages. Unbelievably, she was released after serving only two years in prison, this was put down to good behaviour, but probably had something to do with her new found fame. After her release in 1994, she began to make many public appearances. Melissa claimed that "no one knew I was a battered woman", and she encouraged others in similar circumstances to speak out and get help. She became a very well-known figure in the media throughout the 1990s. Popular opinion, influenced by Melissa's emotionally charged story, was that the killing of Stewart was a heroic act.

Towards the end of the 1990s, Melissa decided that she wanted a fresh start. She moved to Florida, and began attending a local Church. That was where, in the year 2000, she met Robert Friedrich.

Robert Friedrich was another vulnerable man, whose wife of 53 years had died in 1999. When he met Melissa, he was 82. In his younger years, Friedrich had been a very successful engineer and inventor. His life savings were estimated to be around $300000, he also owned his house, and had several insurance policies. Friedrich had sons, but they lived quite far away in Boston. Friedrich was lonely, and had been struggling to cope with the loss of his beloved wife. Melissa claimed that when she saw Friedrich at Church, the Holy Spirit spoke to her and told her that he would be her next husband. Only three days after meeting, Melissa and Friedrich were engaged.

Friedrich's family were concerned. His son, Dennis, and daughter in law, Karen, say that at first they were cautiously optimistic, thinking perhaps it would be good for Friedrich to have some company. However, when marriage was mentioned so quickly, it set off alarm bells. Friedrich wanted his son's approval to marry Melissa, but Dennis refused to give it. His main concern was that she could be a gold digger. In the end, the outcome was much worse.

Despite his family encouraging him not to rush, Friedrich married Melissa having known her for less than one month. Melissa acquired another name, Melissa Ann Friedrich. The wedding took place in secret, in Dartmouth, Nova Scotia. Dennis Friedrich was very angry with his father, but there was little he could do other than cross his fingers and hope that the marriage would be a happy one.

The newlyweds set off on the honeymoon of a lifetime, which lasted for five months and significantly decreased Friedrich's life savings. On their return, they settled in Bradenton, Florida. According to family members, Friedrich seemed content. Even at 82, he had always been in good health, but after returning to Florida this quickly began to change. He became unsteady on his feet, and fell over several times. A worrying pattern started to emerge. Friedrich would feel dizzy, fall, and end up in hospital. He would then recover quickly and be sent home, only for the same thing to happen again a few days later. Friedrich's son Dennis also noticed that his father often seemed confused on the phone, slurring his words, and not sounding his normal self. Suspicions grew when Friedrich visited Dennis in Boston, and appeared totally fine, almost back to his old self again. Dennis realised that Friedrich only got ill when Melissa was around. The family decided that something needed to be done. Friedrich's other son, Bob, contacted an Elder Abuse Agency in Florida. The agency visited Friedrich at home, and recommended that he should have 24 hour care, to ensure that he was being looked after properly. Melissa refused this care, and even threatened to sue the agency involved. She left a threatening voice mail message for Friedrich's sons, saying that they were being cut out of Friedrich's will and would be left with nothing: "you guys are getting nothing, a big fat zero".

After being married for less than 18 months, in December 2002, Robert Friedrich died of a heart attack. As his wife, Melissa was responsible for making the necessary arrangements following the death. Dennis claims that the doctor who signed the death certificate for Friedrich didn't even see his body in person; he simply took Melissa's word for it over the phone. Melissa organized for Friedrich's body to be cremated extremely quickly after his death, meaning that there was never a chance to conduct an autopsy. Melissa stayed in Florida for about five months. During which time she sold the house and collected various insurance payments, pocketing around $100000. Friedrich's family were left with nothing but sad memories, and pictures.

By 2004, Melissa was back in Prince Edward Island and moving on with her life. But Friedrich's son Dennis was haunted by his father's death. He would regularly type Melissa's name into Google, even trying other names that he knew she had used previously, Melissa Ann Russell, Melissa Ann Shepard, and Melissa Ann Stewart. Finally, he found an article in the Halifax Herald called "Too Many Deaths along Old Guysborough Road". The article covered the killing of Gordon Stewart and Melissa's strange history. At that point, Dennis Friedrich was in little doubt about what was behind his father's fast decline. Dennis is still convinced that Robert Friedrich was poisoned by Melissa. He tried to make a criminal case against her, but it was impossible because no evidence of the crime remained. Dennis has stated that Melissa is "not just a gold digger, she's a murderer".

Melissa has always denied killing Friedrich, claiming that marriage was a very good one and she wouldn't have had any reason to want him dead. She said that she has been "railroaded" and misunderstood, and that these strange happenings were merely coincidences.

During 2004, Melissa was living happily off Friedrich's $100000. But, it turned out that this wasn't her only source of income. Melissa had also been claiming spousal benefits under the names Shepard and Stewart and using different social security numbers. When police discovered this, they set out to arrest her. But, she was gone. By November 2004, Melissa had started travelling back to Florida again, to meet yet another potential victim.

Alex Strategos was 73 years old and lived in Pinellas Park, Florida. He had two previous unsuccessful marriages, and had been living alone for 10 years. Alex Strategos moved to Florida in 2002 to be closer to his son, Dean. Strategos had developed some health problems; he was diabetic and experienced a stroke. Despite the health issues, Strategos was happy in Florida. Family friend Judi Frock said that he seemed fine, but wasn't very talkative, spending a lot of time on the computer. Judi Frock and Dean Strategos both wanted him to meet someone, they didn't realise that he already had- over the internet.

Melissa first contacted Alex Strategos on the 6th of October 2004, she saw his profile on a Christian dating website, and sent him a message. They discussed how she had used to live very close to Strategos' home, but that she had moved back to Prince Edward Island after becoming widowed. After less than four weeks of messaging, Melissa suggested a visit. She said that she would drive down to Florida from Canada, around 2000 miles. Strategos asked where she was planning to stay; he warned her that he only had one bedroom. Melissa wasn't fazed by this. In fact, she seemed very keen.

When Strategos mentioned the upcoming visit to his son Dean and family friend, Judi Frock, they were very surprised. They both thought it was a little strange that a woman would be willing to drive so far alone and stay with someone on the first meeting. However, they were happy that Strategos had met someone, and wanted to be supportive. Melissa made the long drive down to Florida.

On her arrival, Melissa and Strategos went out for a long, romantic meal. After they had finished dining, they returned to his condo. Melissa opened a bottle of wine and brought Strategos a glass. When it got late, Strategos offered to sleep on the couch, but Melissa refused this, saying that she wanted to sleep with him. During the night, Alex Strategos woke up feeling unwell. He tried to make his way to the bathroom, but was overcome with dizziness and passed out. Strategos had no idea that this mysterious illness had proved very common among Melissa's previous husbands too.

Alex Strategos was admitted to hospital on the night of his first meeting with Melissa. She told hospital staff that she was his wife. She also took his house keys, saying that she would keep the place nice for him. With Strategos still in the hospital, Melissa went back to his house and made herself at home. Dean Strategos visited Melissa at the house, saying that his father had sent him to see how she was doing. Melissa was surprised; she hadn't known that Strategos had a son. The first impression that Dean Strategos got was that she seemed nice -

classy and polite. Dean had been worried that Melissa was just after his father's money. But, after their first meeting and seeing Melissa's white Cadillac, his fears subsided. It seemed like she had plenty of money of her own, so why would she need to steal any from Alex Strategos?

After a few days in hospital, Strategos seemed to recover. Doctors couldn't find a reason for his collapse, so they sent him home. Melissa promised to care for him and she appeared to be doing a good job. The house was always kept spotless, and Strategos said that she was an excellent cook. Dean Strategos and Judi Frock visited the couple, and found a very pleasant scene. Everything seemed to be working out fine. Alex Strategos started to talk about marriage, even though he had only known Melissa for a couple of months.

Less than a week passed before Strategos was admitted to hospital again, and a familiar pattern emerged. Over the following two months, Alex Strategos was rushed to hospital a further seven times. Dean was worried about his father's health. But, initially he didn't suspect Melissa, he was actually glad that she was there keeping an eye on Alex. It was family friend, Judi Frock, who had doubts. She thought the whole situation was very odd, and noticed that Alex Strategos always got more ill when he was around Melissa. She mentioned this to her work colleagues, one of whom was the wife of a local police officer. Frock's colleague called her husband, Mike Lynch, and told him what had been going on. The story raised several red flags for Lynch, and he decided to look into it further.

Meanwhile, nurses moved Strategos into a 24 hour nursing home, so that he could be monitored properly. Melissa lied to nurses at the home, saying that she was Strategos' wife. She then tried to get him a permanent place at the home, without consulting either Alex Strategos himself, or his son Dean. A nurse told Dean this information, along with the shocking revelation that Melissa had also made Strategos sign a power of attorney document whilst he was very ill. Melissa was now in control of all Strategos' property and finances. This alarmed Dean, and he realised that something was very wrong.

Mike Lynch began his investigation by talking to Alex Strategos. Strategos told Lynch that he couldn't remember any of the times he had passed out, this felt very different to any medical problems he had previously experienced. Initially, Strategos didn't want to believe that Melissa could be behind his illness, until Lynch looked at his blood work and found something very strange. There were relatively high levels of benzodiazepine, a powerful tranquilizer, in Strategos' blood. Strategos had never been prescribed sedatives. Mike Lynch had seen benzodiazepine being used as a recreational drug, so he knew what the effects were – dizziness, confusion, and collapsing. Strategos told Lynch that every night before bed Melissa would bring him a small bowl of his favourite ice cream. Lynch believed that this was how Melissa was getting him to ingest the drug.

The next move was to look for a motive, and Lynch found one quickly. Melissa had made several large bank transfers from Strategos' account to her own. Overall, there was around $18000 missing. Dean and Alex Strategos were both horrified when they heard this news. There was no doubt left in their minds that Melissa was up to no good. After further investigation they discovered Melissa's other names, and her dark past. The police arrested her, and found a large stash of benzodiazepine and other prescription drugs in her possession. Luckily for Melissa, they couldn't prosecute her for attempted murder because the levels of benzodiazepine in Strategos' blood were not high enough to kill him. Instead, she was convicted of several charges including exploiting the elderly, forgery, and theft. She was sentenced to five years in jail. Melissa denies any wrong doing, maintaining that the missing money was used on Strategos' request to pay bills and look after the house. Alex Strategos described Melissa as "cold-blooded", saying that she tricked and deceived him. Dean made up the name the "internet black widow", a name that has stuck, and with good reason.

Melissa was released in 2009, a year early. Eventually, she headed back to Canada and moved into a retirement complex near New Glasgow. Melissa had family connections in the area. People assumed that as a relatively elderly lady, Melissa's black widow days would be over. But, this proved to be far from the truth. In September 2012, a man named Fred Weeks received a visit from a neighbour, who introduced herself as Millie Ann Russell.

Fred Weeks was another widower, 75 years of age. In his working days he had been a teacher, and was described as a very kind man. Weeks and Melissa shared a whirlwind romance, and they married on the 25th September 2012 in New Glasgow, just two weeks after they first met. The marriage was conducted by an old friend of Weeks, Justice of the Peace, George Megeney. Megeney said that "they were happy at that time, or at least Fred was, and Millie appeared to be". However, the Justice of the Peace began to have serious doubts about Millie after a friend recognised her, and revealed her former identity. George Megeney contacted the police, but as no crime had been committed, they were powerless to act.

Weeks and Melissa went on a short honeymoon to Newfoundland. They were there for four days, before heading to North Sydney, a ferry terminal town on the route back to New Glasgow. When booking a room at a bed and breakfast, Melissa informed the owner, Cheryl Chambers, that they were both a little travel sick and needed to rest. Cheryl Chambers noticed that "Mr Weeks didn't look well at all", describing his appearance as gaunt. Whereas Mrs Weeks, Melissa, looked healthy, well-groomed even, in a red suit. This struck Chambers as odd, and she decided to keep an eye on the elderly couple. Later that evening she knocked on the door to check on them. Melissa answered and told her that everything was fine, they were just resting. Chambers could see Mr Weeks on the bed, still looking very ill, she was concerned.

In the morning, Chambers asked Melissa if there had been any improvement in Mr Weeks' condition. When she heard that the answer was no, she offered to call an ambulance. Melissa said yes, but that she would like to finish eating her breakfast and get ready first. This alarmed Chambers, who called an ambulance immediately. Fred Weeks was taken to hospital, where Melissa informed the doctor that he had no children and that he had been prescribed tranquilizers – these statements were of course false. Luckily, the hospital staff had access to his medical records, and realised that she was lying. They called the police. Melissa had already made her way back home to New Glasgow. People began to make the connection, news spread and the media debated the possibility that the internet black widow had struck again.

Melissa was charged with attempted murder, but again the charge didn't stick. Even though police knew how dangerous Melissa was, they couldn't prosecute her without sufficient evidence. The judge accepted her guilty plea for failing to provide the necessities of life and administering a noxious substance. In 2013, the 78 year old was sentenced to three and a half years in jail.

Luckily, Fred Weeks recovered. He understood that it was all lies and that Melissa had tried to kill him. "She was good at it, got to give her that" remarked Weeks.

On the 18th of March 2016, a white haired Melissa was released from prison. The terms for her release included not being allowed any access to the internet whatsoever, and having to inform the police if she started any romantic relationships, so that the man in question could be warned about her history.

Less than one month later, on the 11th of April 2016, Melissa was spotted by a community police officer at Halifax Central Library. The officer approached, and discovered that Melissa was accessing the internet. He also found a device in her possession that could be used to get online. These were breaches of Melissa's release conditions, so she was arrested again. On the 4th of August 2016, her lawyers entered not guilty pleas for all the charges, with her trial set to take place early 2017. However, on the 22nd of December 2016, all charges against Melissa were dropped.

Melissa's luck seems to be never ending. Despite having had a hand in two deaths, and poisoning a further two men, she has spent a surprisingly short amount of time in jail. Chief Justice Joseph Philip Kennedy advised that "people who have contact with this lady should be very careful". There is no reason to believe that Melissa has changed her ways, in fact the opposite is likely. Single, elderly men beware; the internet black widow is still on the hunt.

WENDI ANDRIANO

Chapter 1

A dying husband needs a devoted wife. But when love runs out, marriage becomes a burden.

On October 8, 2000, Wendi Andriano snapped. She had played the part of devoted wife to her terminally ill husband, Joe Andriano, for years, but when the love left their marriage, so did Wendi's patience for her husband's eventual demise.

Wendi had a plan to help nudge nature along, and when her plan b expired, she took matters directly into her own hands and bludgeoned him to death.

Wendi first tried to poison her husband by spiking his last meal, a homemade beef stew, with sodium azide, but Joe Andriano did not ingest enough to kill him, only enough to vomit it back up. Wendi then grabbed the nearest object, a bar stool, and beat her dying husband over the head so many times that parts of his brain became exposed.

After thinking she had successfully killed her husband twice, Wendi then realized that Joe was still breathing, so she took a knife from the family kitchen and stabbed him in the side of the throat.

Minutes later, Joe was finally dead.

This bizarre and frantic way Wendi killed her husband isn't the strangest thing about the case though. Known even to Wendi, Joe was due to die from terminal cancer within the next few years anyways.

Why Wendi couldn't wait to kill her husband is an intriguing tale wrought with sex, lies, and strangely, a lack of patience.

Chapter 2

Wendi and Joe Andriano grew up together in the small farming community of Casa Grande, Arizona. But while they both had gone to the same school, they never dated. As a minister's daughter, Wendi's social life was restricted to her father's church. Her celebration for graduating high school was even in the form of a missionary trip to

Mexico in 1989. When she returned she took a job at the local clerical hospital.

Wendi met Joe in 1992 through friends. Although when the couple started dating Joe's family found the minister's daughter to be an unusual fit for the loud, outgoing former football player, they all thought she was friendly enough and approved of the match.

Joe worked for a local boat builder. He was very mechanically inclined and was a very good welder. He owned his own boat and took Wendi for several cruises around the local hot spots for speedboats. They were inseparable.

The couple married in January of 1994. Their wedding took place in a baptist church across the street from their shared elementary school. Their reception was at the Elk's club and was populated by their many friends and family. Even after two years of dating, though, Joe's family felt like they didn't know his new bride very well, but Joe seemed to be very happy, so they were happy for him.

Soon after marrying, the couple became business partners when they started a small company that did windshield repair and replacement. The business combined Wendi's office experience with Joe's mechanical experience, skills they both exceeded at, and the business thrived.

The couple hadn't been married a whole year yet before they faced their first major challenge together. That fall, Joe noticed an odd bump on his neck. When he had it tested, he was told it was a non-cancerous benign tumor, but it wasn't long before they were second-guessing the diagnoses. A year after it was removed, the tumor grew back.

A second surgery and round of tests seemed to reconfirm that the tumor was benign, but shortly after Wendi gave birth to a son in 1997, the tumor was back yet again.

The third time the tumor returned, Joe's wife and family were convinced that the tumor had to be cancer. This fear was confirmed in 1998 when Joe underwent surgery to have the bump removed for the fourth time. Joe's pre-surgery chest x-ray showed that not only was the tumor cancerous, but that the cancer had now spread across Joe's throat, chest, and lungs.

The prognosis wasn't good—Joe had a rare form of cancer and while radiation and chemotherapy were standard, there was no guarantee they would work. On top of this, Wendi was also pregnant again and was only months away from giving birth to the couple's second child.

Chapter 3

In an effort to increase Joe's chances of survival while decreasing his suffering, Wendi and Joe decided to pursue holistic treatments before resorting to chemotherapy and radiation. They had been told that chemotherapy and radiation treatments would likely not cure Joe, but they would lengthen his life by a few years; however, these years would be anything from pleasant. The horrific side-effects chemotherapy and radiation treatments cause are well known.

So the Andriano's decided first to try anything from special diets to alternative medical treatments to prayer—anything that had a chance to help Joe. Joe even attended a holistic treatment centre for cancer patients in Colorado for a few weeks where he was surrounded by other men and women facing the same prognosis as him. After seeing the bravery of others in the same position as him, Joe began thinking about his future again and began to see it as bright for the first time in a while.

After Joe returned from his holistic healing getaway with a bright new attitude, the Andriano's decided the next best step would be for Joe to begin chemotherapy treatments. He had begun to crave his future and was ready to take steps to achieve it. Unfortunately, taking these steps meant that Joe needed to quit his welding job as well as his own position in the couple's business.

To help make ends meet, Wendi returned to working for the first time since the birth of the couple's children. She ended up taking multiple jobs and worked long hours while continuing to care for her husband at home. Eventually, Wendi landed a job managing the San Riva apartment complex in the Ahwatukee foothills, an upscale neighbourhood outside of Phoenix.

Wendi's new job came with some major perks—the salary was above average, which was nice as Wendi was now the family's breadwinner, and it required Wendi to live on site, which meant that the family now lived in a luxury apartment but paid no rent. Wendi's new job also gave her a new life. A large part of her duties as complex manager was arranging social activities for the other residents of the San Riva apartments, who were mostly young, wealthy, single businesspeople.

Every Saturday the complex hosted picnics, pool parties, or late-night socials. The residents even had their own baseball team. Wendi was required to attend every event, which meant Joe was needed to stay home with their two children. Wendi enjoyed this alone time so much that many of the residents at the San Riva had no clue she had a dying husband and two children at home. She partied like she was single.

The first few months at the San Riva went well. Wendi organized mixers and pool parties for the tenants while Joe took care of the kids. Despite being very weak from treatments, he did everything he could, he wanted to do it. He prefered to have his kids around him even when he didn't feel good.

Although they had never gotten close to their daughter-in-law, Joe's parents also pitched in with babysitting so the couple could have time alone together. They didn't get to see each other much as Wendi began spending more and more time at work. Her new job had also given her a new confidence, and she spent many nights out on the town dancing and drinking away her weekday stress with friends. Joe began to fear that Wendi would soon leave him for her new lifestyle, but this fear got sidetracked when his health continued to fail.

In the summer of 2000, when tests revealed his cancer had spread yet again, Joe and Wendi decided to increase the frequency of Joe's chemotherapy. Joe agreed to undergo more treatments, but they quickly took their toll. He lost 15 pounds in the first week alone, and Joe's doctor became concerned. It went from bad to worse very quickly.

By the beginning of October 2000, it became harder and harder to remain optimistic about Joe's chances of beating his cancer. It became apparent it was terminal, but doctors insisted that with treatment Joe could live for several more years.

No one had any idea that Joe would be dead after only the first week of the month. No one, that is, except for one person—Wendi Andriano.

Chapter 4

Just after 2:00 a.m. on October 8, Wendi Andriano called a friend who also lived in the San Riva apartment complex. She told her friend that she needed someone to stay with the kids while she took Joe to the hospital. When the friend arrived, she found Joe on the floor, barely alive.

Joe was on the floor in the fetal position. There was vomit on the floor around him and he couldn't stand up. Wendi confided in her friend that she told Joe that she had called 9-1-1 and paramedics were on the way, but this wasn't true. After seeing Joe in such poor condition, the neighbour urged Wendi to call paramedics. She then went outside to wait for them to arrive while Wendi waiting with her husband.

Wendi did call 9-1-1, but when the EMT's arrived minutes later, she refused to let them or her friend inside the apartment. She said that her husband was dying from terminal cancer and had a do not resuscitate order. Joe was not to receive any medical attention.

Just over an hour later, at 3:30 a.m., Wendi dialed 9-1-1 a second time. The same team of paramedics came to the house. It didn't take them long to realize something wasn't quite right, so they contacted the police department. Both the paramedics and the police were shocked to find out that Joe, who had been terminally ill from cancer for quite some time had died, but not from the cancer that had been slowly killing his body. He died from being repeatedly beaten with a bar stool and from being stabbed in the neck.

When the police opened the front door of the apartment, they were confronted with obvious signs of a deadly struggle. The apartment was in a complete state of disarray, and there was blood everywhere. Blood had been traced throughout the kitchen, the dining room, and the living room of the luxury apartment, and blood had spattered across the walls the ceilings. Lying in the middle of the bloody scene was Joe, with a knife wound in his neck and holes spattered across his visible skull.

While crime scene technicians surveyed the apartment, phoenix police took Wendi down to the station for a formal statement. She was wearing clothes drenched in Joe's blood and was armed with a story that explained how Joe's death had been a complete accident.

In the interrogation room, Wendi told police she and joe had spent the evening in Casa Grande visiting with Joe's parents. They put the kids to bed after they returned home, which was when Joe noticed something odd about Wendi's appearance—she wasn't wearing her wedding ring.

According to Wendi, Joe worked himself into a rage and began accusing her of having an affair. This argument turned into a shoving match, and when Joe grabbed a belt, Wendi grabbed a bar stool and swung. Joe went down on all fours so she hit him again. It was then that she called her neighbour for help. Joe may have been in a terrible state when the neighbour saw him, but according to Wendi when she went outside Joe had gotten back to his feet easily.

Wendi said she denied the EMTs access to the apartment because she and Joe were both embarrassed about the fight, but just minutes after the EMTs left, the fight got physical again.

Wendi said that her husband tried to strangle her with a telephone cord and she defended herself with the first weapon she could get in her hands—a kitchen knife. She was vague about how the knife ended up in Joe's neck though, saying she was holding the knife up when Joe suddenly fell flat on his face. The next thing she knew, blood was spurting everywhere. He must have fallen on the blade, it was simply an accident.

Many things about this story didn't make sense to the police. First of all, the timeline presented in Wendi's story didn't match the accounts of Wendi's neighbour or the EMTs. Wendi's neighbour had seen no evidence of a physical fight when they first entered the apartment—there were no broken bar stools or blood like later when the police arrived. As well, Wendi had few injuries on her body, definitely no injuries that would necessitate self defence in the form of murder.

Joe's illness also shed doubt on Wendi's story. Joe's parents told police that when the Andriano's visited earlier that evening, Joe had been so weak from his treatments that he could barely stand. They had spent the evening doting on their sick son, bringing him any comforts he wanted. If he was too weak to stand, he certainly couldn't have been strong enough to violently attack Wendi.

Police also uncovered a damning piece of evidence from Wendi herself, in a moment when she thought she was all alone. The investigators that had been questioning Wendi left her on her own in the interrogation room for some time while they fact checked some of her statements and checked in with the investigators who were scanning the crime scene for evidence. During this time, Wendi made a phone call to a coworker at the apartment complex and asked them to hide some of her files from the police. This immediately led to a search of Wendi's office where police found evidence that Wendi had in fact killed her husband. She had even been planning it for months.

Chapter 5

While both investigators strongly believed that Wendi Andriano was responsible for Joe's death, they were stumped by her motive. Why would Wendi kill her dying husband? The police didn't know, but they did have one intriguing lead—the phone call Wendi had made from the interrogation room. They were determined to find out what she was trying to hide.

When they searched her office, police discovered that Wendi had been disciplined at work for using her computer to search inappropriate items on the internet while on the clock.She had been conducting research on poisons, and how to use certain poisons to kill people. They also discovered the papers that she had tried to hide—shipping notices for a substance known as sodium azide.

Sodium azide is a lethal substance with a variety of industrial uses including propelling airbags. It is not, however, something that the average person can simply go out and buy. It's not restricted to the point where only certain companies can possess it, but it needs to be bought for a reason—something that an apartment complex didn't have. But based on the information on the shipping invoice, Wendi had found a way around that.

Wendi had created a fictitious business license using the tax ID form for the apartment complex. Using a Xerox machine and an exacto knife, Wendi had removed all information specific to the apartment complex and inserted fictitious information for a fake company.

The business name on the shipping notice was bogus, but the address wasn't. Wendi had the substance delivered to an address in Scottsdale, Arizona in an attempt to distance herself, but that plan didn't work. When the police tracked down the real address on the invoice, workers at the company positively identified Wendi as the person who had come by a couple weeks earlier to pick up a package she had mistakenly had shipped there instead of her own office.

Wendi's coworkers had seen her with a package but that she had been very mysterious with the contents. She refused to tell anyone what was inside. Had this been the sodium azide? And if so, where was it now?

Chapter 6

Suspecting that Wendi had tried to poison Joe with the sodium azide, police took samples of every medication and food they could find in the Andriano's apartment. If Joe had ingested poison, it would have explained the awful state Wendi's friend had seen him in just over an hour before he died. Luckily, the remainders of Joe's last supper, homemade beef stew, still sat in a pot on the stove.

However, police didn't find any evidence of Wendi's mysterious package, or any evidence of the sodium azide itself in Wendi and Joe's apartment. They had just begun to lose hope in finding the poison when they found out Wendi had a storage space in the building that she failed to tell the police about. Hidden behind a stack of boxes in Wendi's storage unit was a small bottle of white powder and a measuring spoon. The white powder was soon identified as sodium azide.

But the storage unit wasn't the only place investigators found the lethal substance—it was also in Joe's stomach contents and in the beef stew on the stove.

While discovering the poison helped police understand that Wendi had been trying to kill her husband, it didn't explain why she had bludgeoned him to death on October 8, 2000. Wendi had spent a lot of time researching poisons and she spent a lot of time manufacturing documents so that she could purchase the poison. It certainly wasn't a spur of the moment decision.

But why would Wendi beat and stab her husband if she had already poisoned him? Prosecutors had a theory, one that would cut to the heart of the crime. It was patience—or more precisely, Wendi's lack of it—that had killed Joe in the end.

Wendi had grown tired of waiting for the cancer to kill Joe, so she decided to give nature a little nudge by poisoning his supper. But according to the theory, when Wendi gave Joe the poison, things didn't go quite to plan. Joe hadn't ingested enough poison to kill him when he began vomiting it back up. With her plan quickly failing, Wendi panicked. She snapped.

Now improvising, Wendi beat Joe with the nearest object she could get her hands on—a bar stool. Pathologists were able to conclude that Wendi beat Joe over the head with the stool no less than twenty-four times. This beating did render Joe unconscious, but still didn't kill him so Wendi grabbed a kitchen knife and stabbed him in the part of his body that caused all this trouble in the first place—the side of his neck.

Chapter 7

Ten days after she murdered her husband, Wendi Andriano was formally charged with first degree murder. Wendi's crime was viewed as being especially cruel due to the large amount of suffering Joe had had to endure over several hours thanks to Wendi's actions. Because of this, the prosecutor's on Wendi's trial did the almost unthinkable, they sought the death penalty.

When Wendi a walked into the Arizona courtroom on September 9, 2004 she looked vastly different from the perky apartment manager that the residents of the San Riva apartments used to know.

At the time of the killing she had been blonde, she had short hair, and generally appeared to be much younger and cute than the individual who appeared in court with long dark hair and thick glasses. Previously, she had liked to look good and show her figure so her conservative dress at the trial was certainly different from the look her friends were used to seeing. She was trying to look more conservative, more innocent.

She had had plenty of time to perfect her new look—it had taken prosecutors almost four years to bring the case to trial. It had been postponed about 12 times before it was finally brought before a judge and jury.

In their opening statement, prosecutors reminded the jury that at the time of the murder Wendi had been anything but the perfect mother or wife she claimed to have been. She had been someone who had no disregard for her husband at all. While her husband was dying, she had gone out partying and started affairs, and when his condition worsened, and it began to cramp her style, she turned to poison.

Wendi didn't like her new role as family breadwinner, especially with the loss of Joe's income, and with rising medical bills, the family was in the worst financial state they had ever been in. Wendi had thought she was going to be able to be a stay-at-home-mom for the rest of her life, and she did not adjust well to her return to the workforce. So Wendi had found an out.

Although Joe did not have any life insurance, even though Wendi had asked several friends to pretend to be Joe in medical exams so he could be insured, Joe had filed a malpractice suit against his former doctor who had continually told him his tumor was benign when it was in fact spreading throughout his body. If Joe died and the lawsuit went through, Wendi would likely walk away with a multi-million dollar settlement.

More than money though, Wendi had wanted freedom. She wanted the freedom to be single again, she wanted freedom to the ball-and-chain who was slowly dragging her spirit into his grave along with himself. Wendi wanted to not have to care about her dying husband anymore, who was too weak to provide her with any love.

Wendi maintained her plea of innocence throughout the trial, and her defence team attempted to prove she had been the victim of abuse not only on the night of Joe's death but also throughout the couple's entire marriage. To explain the poison, Wendi told the court that Joe had been the one who had grown tired of waiting for the cancer to end his life, and had asked Wendi to help him do it himself.

On the witness stand Wendi said that Joe had willingly taken the poison, but she also stuck by the story that she had originally told police, that Joe had suspected an affair and became enraged when she affirmed them. He became deranged and attacked her, starting the bloody fight. Wendi claimed Joe had died during the ensuing struggle.

Wendi's story wasn't enough to convince the court though, and on November 18, 2004 she was found guilty of the crime. It had taken the jury only two-and-a-half-hours to come to its unanimous decision. Six years after her husband joe had been diagnosed with terminal cancer, Wendi Andriano faced a possible death sentence of her own.

On December 20, 2004, the jurors assigned to Wendi Andriano's case met and decided on Wendi's fate—it would be death for Ms Andriano. Wendi, along with most of the courtroom, was aghast. Even Joe's family was shocked by the decision. Wendi Andriano became the second ever woman to be put on death row in Arizona, a state that reserves the death penalty for the worst of the worst.

Wendi Andriano has since attempted to appeal the court's decision, but as of early 2017, all attempts have been denied and Wendi continues to wait on death row. Wendi and Joe's children now live with Joe's parents, who continue to mourn the loss of their beloved son.

Joe Andriano's death was especially long, and especially cruel, but no happy ending was found when Wendi was sentenced to her own death. Many view the conclusion of this case to be the saddest possible outcome. On October 8, 2000, two lives were lost, and two children were left without parents.